Praise for *The Gate of Memory*

"Out of the wreckage of the camps, these poets have created lasting objects of beauty, sorrow and rage. *The Gate of Memory* is a landmark anthology to be read and reread."
—Julie Otsuka, author of *When the Emperor Was Divine*

"*The Gate of Memory* makes the familiar strange—and incarceration should be strange, even unimaginable. Perhaps poetry inoculates us against normalization. My family spoke of internment, and I thought this was particular to a small and dwindling we. To move through *The Gate of Memory*, however, is to imagine a we that is still gathering strength, the we who closed Rikers, made San Quentin a museum, and awoke from the fascist fever dream of mass deportation and incarceration."
—Naomi Murakawa, author of *The First Civil Right: How Liberals Built Prison America*

"A vital ancestral fire tended by brilliant poets, *The Gate of Memory* offers us so many profound and devastating glimpses into the precise contours of incarceration and its aftermath. I was struck by the myriad inflections of silence, care and resistance that descendants share with such discernment and fortitude. Through attentive witness and tenacious solidarity, this book actively metabolizes trauma, transforming some of the pain and injustice into collective strength. This offering of intergenerational love stunned me with its depth and breadth."
—Rita Wong, author of *Current, Climate: The Poetry of Rita Wong*

"This pilgrimage of poems, blessed by elder poets Mitsuye Yamada and Lawson Inada, is here gifted at *The Gate of Memory*. Our parents, who once named that memory ambiguously "camp," have passed beyond that gate. May these words render solace, rise as haunting stars to light our way."
—Karen Tei Yamashita, author of *Letters to Memory*

THE GATE OF MEMORY

Poems by Descendants of Nikkei Wartime Incarceration

• • • • • • • • • • • • •

edited by Brynn Saito and Brandon Shimoda

with a foreword by Mitsuye Yamada

Haymarket Books
Chicago, Illinois

Published in 2025 by
Haymarket Books
P.O. Box 180165
Chicago, IL 60618
www.haymarketbooks.org

ISBN: 979-8-88890-371-1

Distributed to the trade in the US through Consortium Book Sales and Distribution (www.cbsd.com) and internationally through Ingram Publisher Services International (www.ingramcontent.com).

This book was published with the generous support of Lannan Foundation, Wallace Action Fund, and Marguerite Casey Foundation.

Special discounts are available for bulk purchases by organizations and institutions. Please email info@haymarketbooks.org for more information.

Cover artwork by Rob Sato, "A New Sound." Risograph print on speckletone paper.

Cover design by Brett Neiman.

Printed in Canada by union labor.

Library of Congress Cataloging-in-Publication data is available.

10 9 8 7 6 5 4 3 2 1

Table of Contents

II. This Is Not the Whole Story

III. Each Leaf / Remembers

IV. I Can Hold My Breath for Years

V. Be Strong Now

Mitsuye Yamada

●●●●●●●●●●●●

Foreword

At 101 years old, I am honored to be asked to write a foreword to this impressive body of work. I do chuckle at the notion that I am one of the "ancestors" to these descendants.

I was just a teenager when I was sent to Minidoka in 1942. I scribbled notes and penned some poems in camp, but I did not think of my experience in terms of its literary or historical value. After the war, like so many of the other "ancestors" referenced in these pages, I normalized my experience as much as possible. I kept quiet and moved on. So decades later, when I began processing my own experiences through poetry, I realized there was no standard blueprint to follow. Indeed, it took me a number of years to think about my experiences through the lens of injustice. By the time I was published, it seemed few people had even heard of the incarceration camps.

The Gate of Memory: Poems by Descendants of Nikkei Wartime Incarceration is a treasure trove of writings by Nikkei poets and writers reflecting on the incarceration experiences of their family members during World War II. Brynn Saito and Brandon Shimoda, editors of this extraordinary collection, have compiled a staggering amount of material that answers a seemingly simple question, "How has the legacy of the incarceration impacted your life?"

This anthology gathers a wide breadth of voices and reflections on a unified subject, offering a myriad of themes and ideas as diverse as the voices that share them. These writers offer fragments of their family stories; a thoughtful documentation of survivors' denial, anger, grief and triumphs passed down through generations, capturing an array of experiences from the profoundly emotional to mundane day-to-day life.

What a relief it is to see these poets capturing the stories from the past so beautifully and empathetically. Their perspectives each add a fresh layer to the story, because this legacy reverberates so personally in their own lives.

I am so impressed at how insightful and outspoken the descendant generations are. While many of my generation typically dealt with our experience of incarceration by keeping silent, these generations are far more skilled at channeling their outrage. They see the connection of the injustices of the past and, in turn, the injustices they see today.

As time creeps further and further away from WWII, it is all the more critical to remember the legacy of our history. *The Gate of Memory* deeply honors these stories.

Brynn Saito and Brandon Shimoda

•••••••••••••

Even the Dead Will Hear Us Speak

It feels like many lifetimes ago and as recently as yesterday that our ancestors—our parents and grandparents and great-grandparents, our aunts and uncles and great-aunts and great-uncles, approaching 150,000 of them—were, during the Second World War, criminalized by the governments of North America, of Canada and the United States, dispossessed of their belongings and livelihoods, forced from their homes, and exiled and incarcerated in prisons and concentration camps across the continent. The story of the mass incarceration of the Nikkei population—the Japanese and Okinawan American and Canadian people—has been told many times, in many ways, in many settings, under many circumstances. Yet it still feels as though the reality of it has not been liberated, or not entirely, from a kind of obscurity that requires the story to be constantly retold.

And so, *many lifetimes ago*: because that is how incarceration, the hard fact of years encircled by barbed wire and wilderness, is often imagined and expressed, including within families of people who were there, including by survivors, who are, as of now, passing away—as a memory that has become increasingly difficult to retrieve and reinhabit. Many of us grew up in the illusion of that distance. The memory, shared through stories, materialized in fragments or like dusting fog off a photograph. Many of us grew up with an awareness of what happened; the story was part of our lives, was talked about openly, and shaped our understanding of the world and how it worked. The meeting ground between knowledge and unknowing formed a piece of the heart of the post-incarceration community, in which the wartime experience, in the ways it has been received or not, in the ways it has stayed remote or become a part of the environment, is still being discovered. It is still being felt.

And so, *yesterday*: because awareness and understanding cannot always guard against the forces of traumatic experience and/or the systems of oppression that form the source and scaffolding of that experience. The components that constituted incarceration, and that maintained it, continue to proliferate. We see it in anti-Asian racism, anti-immigrant legislation, migrant detention, family separation; in generalized, pervasive politics of fear; in the internalization of an enforced contest with one's citizenship and sense of self; in the funding and application, by our governments, of these same racial, imperial, colonial, carceral logics on indigenous land and in the streets of the Americas and around the world. We are made to see it whenever incarceration or the camps are invoked by politicians or in the media as an example, a metaphor, or a threat. And we can see these forms of oppression being resisted in the continuously evolving response to these injustices—in acts of vigilance, protest, repair; in intergenerational and intercommunal solidarity; in storytelling and art-making and writing, including poetry.

Nikkei poets across generations and cultures have produced, and are producing, one of the most significant bodies of work to address, illuminate, and redress a single historical event—or, more accurately, a structure—in all of its complexities. Poetry has formed an essential record of the Nikkei wartime incarceration, one that complements and often exceeds what the historical record is able to illuminate. We can read this record in the vast body of poetry that precedes the work that appears in this anthology: poetry written by the survivor generations, to which this anthology owes an immeasurable debt. We can read this record in the poems, written in Japanese, by Issei in Hawaiʻi, collected in Jiro and Kay Nakano's *Poets Behind Barbed Wire*, which begins, in translation, "The time has come / For my arrest." We can read it in the Kaiko haiku collected in Violet Kazue de Cristoforo's *May Sky: There Is Always Tomorrow* and in the poems published, often in Japanese, in literary journals and anthologies in the camps—*Cactus Blossoms* (written by high school students) in Gila River, *Heart Mountain Bungei* in Heart Mountain, *Reiko* and *Yamabiko* in Tashme, *Tessaku* in Tule Lake, among many others. We can read it in poems by Lawson Fusao Inada, Lonny Kaneko, Joy Kogawa, Lawrence Matsuda, Janice Mirikitani, Roy Miki, James Masao Mitsui, Takeo Ujo Nakano, Kinori Oka, Sukeo Sameshima, Toyo Suyemoto, and Mitsuye Yamada, among many others. (It is important to note that many of the poets who were in camp were incarcerated as young children or were born there, so although they are survivors, their experience and therefore their poetry correspond, in many ways, with that of a descendant.)

Mitsuye Yamada, who very generously wrote the foreword for this anthology, wrote poems while working the graveyard shift at the hospital in the Minidoka concentration camp in Idaho; some of her poems, which appear in her book *Camp Notes*, were drawn directly from things she saw and heard while working there. They, with poems by all of the poets of the survivor generations, offered a kind of surrogacy, ushering us into a more intimate history of the wartime incarceration: more granular, more tactile, more challenging and complicated, more painful, sometimes even more playful. They have enabled us to see and hear and feel our families on the periphery, moving through daily and nightly life, a few degrees off the margins of that writing. "I dare you to hear me," sings Miya Folick, in the voice of her grandfather ("Song for Kanjitsu"). And it felt, suddenly, with everything we had been given, and with how it had been given to us, like we were returning. Because it occurred to us that part of the deal of our inheritance was to realize, to put together and continue, the experience of those who came before us. And to be witnesses from the future.

Here is one of the many ways this anthology revealed itself. In August of 2017—before our friendship and collaboration—Brandon discovered an audio recording on *Hyphen Magazine*'s website of Brynn reading her poem, "Alma, 1942." The poem—which does not appear in this anthology, but, like so many other poems, is alive in its consciousness—is about Brynn's grandmother, Alma, and her experience being incarcerated in the Gila River concentration camp in Arizona. The poem is in Alma's voice; she alternates between narrating her experience and wondering why Brynn, the curious grandchild, wants to know so much about it. On the recording, Brynn reads the poem fast, as if both rushing into and away from the past, except for the final lines, when she slows down: "You'll see it for yourself / when you go there roving / with your questions for the barracks / like a hungry ghost." Hearing these lines, Brandon thought of his grandfather, Midori, who was incarcerated in a Department of Justice prison in Missoula, Montana, under suspicion of being a spy for Japan. Brandon thought about his relationship to his grandfather's experience; how he too, in the absence of his grandfather, was roving the ruins, asking questions of the barracks, "like a hungry ghost," that is, fatedly, without relief, and for what was beginning to feel like forever. He wrote to Brynn immediately.

Brynn had just cofounded, with the artist and farmer Nikiko Masumoto, Yonsei Memory Project (YMP), an intergenerational, intercultural, arts-based memory-keeping initiative. YMP was beginning to establish programs that put Yonsei and Sansei into conversation with Nisei elders; they had just organized a tour of Japanese American memorials and sites in and around Fresno, as a way to talk about memory and memorialization. "The Nisei shared detailed stories about camp," Brynn wrote back to Brandon, "and the Yonsei expressed gratitude, as many of their grandparents never talked about it." Alma never talked about it. Neither did Midori. What struck Brandon about Brynn's poem is that, in the absence of her grandmother talking about it and in the abundance of wanting to generate a picture out of that absence, Brynn was illuminating the contours of the past; she, the descendant, was beginning to tell the story.

Brandon, meanwhile, was in the early stages of writing a book on incarceration. For part of his research, he devised a questionnaire that he was sharing with descendants. The questions asked about their relationship to their family's experience (when did you first learn about it, who told you, how was it told), as well as more speculative questions about ancestors and dreams. Brandon was also preparing to lead a tour of the prison labor camp on the mountain north of Tucson, where more than forty Nisei men were incarcerated, "with the same intention: to question the barracks," Brandon wrote to Brynn. "Or the ghosts thereof..."

We were both at the beginning of opening spaces in which we could, in fact, ask questions of the barracks, but with the walls pulled down to reveal the truth that there is little to differentiate between inside and outside. We were at the beginning of transforming personal curiosities—by turns melancholic and desperate, animated and meandering—into public reclamations. We were looking for our grandparents, or some repressed or arrested part of them, but we were looking for each other too. Because we were looking for ourselves. This was the beginning of a correspondence that has written itself directly into these pages.

The Gate of Memory is an attempt to illuminate the energy and the diversity, and share the myriad effects and possibilities, of the poetry of descendants. The work is that of eternal return; of pilgrimage, of imagining and reenactment, of reclamation and redemption, of an insatiable need to understand, to ask questions directly of history, to receive and also to reject the answers that are returned. It is portraiture formed out of a balance between uncertainty and conviction, comparison and self-determination. The poetry expresses the complexity of reconstituting the past, while suggesting that to reconstitute the past is not, in the end, the desire or the task, but rather to honor the rites and rituals of remembrance in the present.

Featured in these pages are descendants of people who were incarcerated in the WWII prisons and camps in Canada, Hawaiʻi, the United States, including Japanese American, Okinawan American, Okinawan Canadian, Japanese Canadian, Alaska Native/Tlingit, Japanese, and mixed race Nikkei, together with those who also identify as Anglo, Cantonese, Chinese, Filipino, Jewish, Korean, Latinx, Taiwanese. In addition to being poets, the contributors are also artists, illustrators, educators, filmmakers, park rangers, healers, community organizers, activists, scholars, historians, musicians, composers, nurses, construction workers. The poets range from those in their twenties to those in their seventies. The older poets were influenced by the stories that were told to them by their parents and grandparents, including the stories, as Amy Uyematsu reminds us in her poem "36 Views of Manzanar," "that will never be told." The younger poets are radicalizing form and approach. They suggest, by the fact and the energy of their work, that history is not bound by time, but is an inheritance to which successive generations contribute their own meanings. Nor is the inheritance bound by subject or theme. The afterlife is its own reference and source, its own genesis.

A note on the term Nikkei and its use in this anthology: *Nikkei* refers, generally speaking, to people of Japanese ancestry and their descendants who have emigrated from Japan, i.e. people of the Japanese diaspora. It must be acknowledged and understood, however, that the diversity of identities and filiations, origins and orientations, as represented in and outside of this anthology, cannot be contained by a single designation. *Nikkei* implies, and often enforces, an inherent connection to a common imperialist, nationalist origin, from which many of us are working to free ourselves in our movements forward. For example, the incorporation of people of the Okinawan diaspora into the identity of the Japanese nation-state reinforces and makes even more widespread the violence of colonization. The term *Nikkei* does not undermine this. The coordinated perception of diverse bodies of people as a monolith enabled incarceration. Incarceration was predicated, in part, on this perception. Its carrying out was the cultivation of that perception through policy. In many ways, incarceration formed and enforced a community that did not exist, and that has since been taken for granted as unified. One facet of the afterlife of incarceration, then, is the attempt to understand the nature of community as both an expedient of the imperial, nationalist project and as a space of renewal and possibility.

In putting this anthology together, we accumulated one thousand pages of poetry. In this way, poetry *is* the community. The sheer volume struck us as both miraculous and heartbreaking; that one of the aftereffects of incarceration could be several generations of descendants overwhelmed with such feeling and the inclination to translate it into literature; that an aftereffect of trauma is the birth of a poet. We could not have imagined the extent to which the afterlife was populated by so many poets reading the past into the present, the present into the past, and possibility into the future. We turned to the poets we knew and admired, whose work influenced our own and helped shape our vision of what an anthology might look like. We discovered poets in the pages of literary journals and anthologies, many of which were out-of-print, such as *Ayumi* (1980), *Yoisho* (1983), *The Hawk's Well* (1987), and *Fusion* (1988-1992); in anthologies such as *Paper Doors: An Anthology of Japanese-Canadian Poetry* (eds. Gerry Shikatani and David Aylward, 1981), *The Open Boat: Poems from Asian America* (ed. Garrett Hongo, 1993) and *Premonitions: The Kaya Anthology of New Asian North American Poetry* (ed. Walter Lew, 1995); the Japanese Canadian Artists Directory and "Nikkei Uncovered," traci kato-kiriyama's curation of poetry on *Discover Nikkei*. We relied upon the advice and enthusiasm of our friends. We held an open call for submissions and received work by over 100 poets, all of whom shared, in addition to their poetry, stories about their families. We were hoping to connect with the work of descendant-poets of the more than 2000 people of Japanese ancestry in Mexico, Central and South America (including over 1800 Japanese Peruvians and 250 Japanese Panamanians). Despite our research, which was aided by writers, translators, and scholars of Latin American literature, we were not able to connect with poets who have been making work on this subject. We hope that this anthology will initiate conversations that make such connections possible. We also hope that it inspires other ways of thinking through this diverse and expanding body of work. The poetry that appears in these pages is bolstered by the work that exists beyond it, and is a manifestation of a much larger, unfolding panorama.

The way we have arranged the anthology embodies one possibility among many. It is shaped into five sections, each corresponding, roughly and associatively, to a phase of the condition of being a descendant. The order of the phases is meant to reflect the nature, texture, and evolution of that condition. Each section begins with epigraphs composed of lines from a poem in that section. The opening poem, Anne Yukie Watanabe's "instructions to, 1942"—which takes as its starting point the exclusion orders issued by the Western Defense Command that enforced the removal of "all persons of Japanese ancestry" from 108 "military areas" in the United States—is a reclamation, an announcement of power, and a challenge to history and the future. The poems in sections I and II return us to the sites of incarceration, to the past and to the experience of being there. The poems in section III are haunted by questions asked and unasked, answered and impossible to answer; portraits and memorials to family members and ancestors coalesce through acts of deep listening. The poems in sections IV and V move into a greater awareness and understanding of systemic oppression in the present, seek community in resistance and resistance in community, consider our place in a tradition of care, forge new ecosystems of being, and give thanks and praise to the multifarious sources for being here.

And yet, is this all wishful thinking? Because it does not always happen in this, or any, order. The writer Ruth Sasaki, whose family was incarcerated in the Topaz camp in Utah, compares the process of awareness to "the way a watercolor evolves: a vibrant image gradually comes into focus, layer by layer, light to dark, as shapes, textures, details slowly emerge."* The sentiment is echoed by Katherine Terumi Laubscher in her poem, "Tamatebako": "The stories I was raised on are watercolor translations."

What is it, exactly, that descendants do? We "tap the currents," writes shō yamagushiku, in the pages of this anthology. We "water our memories," writes Amanda Mei Kim. We "pray for our families," writes Paulette "Tkl' Un Yeik" Moreno. We "free the ghosts," writes W. Todd Kaneko. We "sing songs / to keep each other awake," writes traci kato-kiriyama. We "dress

---

* From Ruth's responses to Brandon's aforementioned questionnaire.

ourselves / in shrouds of tule reeds / stitched with barbed wire," writes Garrett Hongo. We "retrace / the forgotten," writes Garrett Kurai. We "dive into the dark," writes Ali Meyers-Ohki. We "inhabit each other," writes Emily Mitamura. "We never arrive alone," writes Lauren Emiko Ito. And as Heather Nagami writes, in the poem "The Gift": "We yearn to hear each other, find each other, to make / our sounds / so heard / that even the dead will hear us speak."

The Gate of Memory

Anne Yukie Watanabe

●●●●●●●●●●●●●●●●

instructions to, 1942

INSTRUCTIONS TO ALL PERSONS WHO
INCARCERATED US
go ahead: put up your posters.
cast your nets. collect us
and send us to camp.

just know that we'll be back.
generations you never dreamed of
will spill into your future.

in a year or two, we'll go on strike.
in 30 years we'll ask our parents why they never told us.
in 40 years we'll testify
against you.

we'll haunt you in the white house,
in our poems
in the streets. we'll fill the streets
with our faces our voices
with cardboard and black paint calling for
abolition
solidarity
an end to borders
the fall of capitalism and freedom for all of us,
not just some of us.

we, the ghosts of the not-yet-born will join Black and Brown
hands

to dig our nails
into the cook county jail
fort sill
berks county detention center
and pull until the roots come loose.

you'll find us hosting open mics
at town halls
in healing circles

you'll find us bringing our young back to manzanar
you'll find us scheming against you on zoom screens
we'll leave *mikans* in the river for our dead babies in
tashme.

in 80 years we'll still be pounding mochi, drinking sake
and filling our pockets
with laughter.

go ahead: fill up our mouths with the taste of shame
a flavor we know so well

each generation we'll spit out young seeds
that have fermented in our cheeks

we'll dig our nails into our families into each other
ourselves

and shake until our spirits come loose.

when the strawberry juice ran down your chin
and we disappeared into barbed wire guard towers
mountains and dust

did you think you'd ever see us again?

was the sugar so sweet you forgot the sugarcane?

just wait. you'll feel our nails digging into you.
we'll fill up your ears with sand
till you hear us from inside of a seashell.

you'll remember us then.

27. no,
28. no.

I
I Bow at the Graves

●●●●●●●

I bow at the graves

I speak to the wind
of my hopes
for
Afterlife
to be a real thing

—traci kato-kiriyama,
"No Redress"

Brynn Saito

●●●●●●●●●

Thirteen Ways of Looking at a Teacher Resource

What types of memories have you inherited?

Stories live in me like sharp lightning flashes across a southern desert.

How have they been passed down to you?

She said: *On the train*
they packed us like sardines
or *We drove our own cars to the camps*
or *I wrote a button*
during the war saying
"I am Korean" for protection.
Then, nothing.
Then great seas of silence
death-quiet and dark
that swallowed us.
Then cans in the backyard
crushed and recognizable.
Then light in a box
rain in a box. Azaleas.

What helps you remember them?

If you get your face quiet enough, what counts as your father's shadow
will speak through it.

How have they impacted your life?

Unknown.

Do you think they've changed over time?

Unknown.

Do any of these inherited memories relate to historical events?

I tell my students: There's no part of you that goes untouched by the angel of history, wings pinned to the air by the storm of progress.

What memories of your own have you chosen to share with others?

The light sings itself awake.
I'm awake at the turn
of the 21st century
and alive to the turning.
Did I ask too large?
I'm afflicted with desire
and the girlhood wish
to lay my body down
in the blue summer grass
lit and unlit by the flicker
of the setting light.
Though shapes and faces
sail down the bloodlines
though ghosts grow their nails
into me, I remain a romantic.
For years, I turned the fire
inward, bleeding to prove
how much I wanted to be here

and break the skin and belong
in ways undreamt by them
to the administered world.

What are the differences between memory and history?

One gives birth to fire and one gives birth to stones.

Do you think history is fixed or objective?

No.

What is the relationship between the past and the present?

Yes.

How do we make meaning from the past?

Yes.

How do you make meaning from the past?

See the writer again at the gate of memory?
See the writer again—
See the writer again at the gate?
Gate the writer again at the memory—
See the past again at the meaning gate?
Past the making, gate the memory—
See the meaning?
She should drown it.

Do you think we have a responsibility to the memories we inherit?

"Even the dead," wrote Walter Benjamin, "will not be safe from the enemy if he wins."

Brian Komei Dempster

Crossing

No turning back. Deep in the Utah desert now, having left one home
to return to the temple of my grandfather. I press the pedal
hard. Long behind me, civilization's last sign—a bent post
and a wooden board: *No food or gas for 200 miles.* The tank

needling below half-full, I smoke Camels to soothe
my worry. Is this where it happened? What's left out there of Topaz
in the simmering heat? On quartzed asphalt I rush

past salt beds, squint at the horizon for the desert's edge: a lone
tower, a flattened barrack, some sign of Topaz—the camp
where my mother, her family, were imprisoned. As I speed
by shrub cactus, the thought of it feels too near,

too close. The engine steams. The radiator
hisses. Gusts gather, wind pushes my Civic side
to side, and I grip the steering wheel, strain to see

through a windshield smeared with yellow jacket wings, blood
of mosquitoes. If I can find it, how much can
I really know? Were sandstorms soft as dreams or stinging
like nettles? Who held my mother when the wind whipped

beige handfuls of her baby cheeks? Was the sand tinged
with beige or orange from oxidized mesas? *I don't remember*
my mother's answer to everything. High on coffee

and nicotine, I half-dream in waves of heat: summon ghosts
from the canyon beyond thin lines of barbed wire. Our name
Ishida. Ishi means stone, *da* the field. We were gemstones
strewn in the wasteland. Only three days

and one thousand miles to go before I reach
San Francisco, the church where my mother was born
and torn away. Maybe Topaz in the desert was long

gone, but it lingered in letters, photos, fragments
of stories. My mother's room now mine, the bed pulled blank
with ironed sheets, a desk set with pen and paper. Here
I would come to understand.

Lauren Emiko Ito

• • • • • • • • • • • •

Infinite Definitions of Birth Right

Is it place
Or people
Or textures
Or graves
Or lullabies caressing cheek
Or. . .

after

thought

Or contorted masks in shapes we can't bring ourselves to recognize
anymore

I hitchhike toward mirages
Count mile markers in what grows beside the road
Who destroys it
How invasive species are named
Where resilient blooms atop fault lines keep extinction at bay

And poetry becomes wills only some can inherit.

Tucking affirmations beneath toes at each bend
I ground prayers for cocooned comfort in given skin
As if we were destined to belong here
After all.

Garrett Hongo

●●●●●●●●●●●

Pilgrimage to the Shrine

Six hours since
the Paradise Cutoff
and running on empty.
No gas stations or rest stops,
no weigh stations, no cops.
Just miles of straight road
and a long double-yellow
unrolling in front of us.

Alan recognizes nothing.
Lawson pops the glove,
pulls out a penlight,
and fingers the map,
pronouncing a few mantras.

Our headlights slide
over a scarecrow
made of tumbleweeds
standing by the road.

He's wearing a kimono,
a dark blue stovepipe hat,
his shoulders cloaked
in a wreath of chrysanthemums.

We pull over,
back up,
and he disappears

into the pale
grey darkness.

It's smoke.
We can smell it,
so somebody's
got to be
close by.

But our eyes
go blind, fill
with tears and ashes
as we stumble
down the offramp.

The smell of
frying trout
and steamed rice
reaches us when
we come to.

An old hermit,
dressed like the scarecrow,
crawls out of his barracks
and brings us tea.

"Drink!" he says,
"It'll pick you up!"
and so we drink
feeling drugged.

Soft blues
in the key
of sleep
suffocates the air.

From up the mountain,

the sound of obsidian
flaking in the wind.
Clouds of black glass
waltz around us.

We dress ourselves
in shrouds of tule reeds
stitched with barbed wire,
stained with salt and mud.

We refuse to cry.

We drift back
to the highway,
holding our fists
like rattles,
shaking them
like bones.

Sharon Hashimoto

●●●●●●●●●●●●●●●

Because You Showed Me a Piece of Barbed Wire

that had lain in the dirt road
beside a lone sign
marking all that remained of barracks,
rowed and eclipsed by the shadow
of Heart Mountain, I thought
of my mother beginning her tour of Japan. What
would she say if she saw me with a piece of her past
cupped in my hand? Would she tell me if the guard tower
rose to her left, perhaps to her right
as she stepped down from the bus,
sleepy and holding her mother's hand?
Or would some things simply remain
unspoken? On the plane, she would be napping,
the pages of a *Sunset Magazine*
fanned by her breath. The small shutters closed,
the movie would flash by, unremembered.
But outside, clouds would buoy up the wings,
buffet the metal. A suitcase in each hand, she'll wait
patiently while my father scowls, passing
through customs under neon signs
she won't understand. Into Tokyo, they'll continue.
I turn the knotted path of wire smelling of ghost dust,
touching the barbs that held everything in.

Reparations: My Mother and Heart Mountain

Unrelenting, the sun breaks down the white paint,
and the slight incline of the barracks' tin roofs

buckles or cracks with the four years
they have weathered. Dust and sweat shine like a cap

of heat on the top of my mother's black head. Grit
chafes her toes; her shoes scratch the rough door.

So I imagine her at thirteen. Her memory blurs
the exact picture with the few facts she can recall,

and I ask her, *What* do *you remember?*
She tells me: *Your grandmother made us think*

it was an adventure to hang blankets at night
and make our own rooms, to fall asleep listening

to the wind and each other's coughing
as floodlights filled the slits in the walls.

Katherine Terumi Laubscher

Tamatebako

Heart Mountain is all sun and stone and wind and shadow.
The grass is tall and as endless as the sky.
The wind tugs at my hair; dust swirls at my boots.
I am here for a pilgrimage; I can walk where I please.

When I look at the rippling wheat fields spread like blankets under the bright blue sky,
I can almost believe it wasn't so terrible, after all.
Flowers bend in the breeze, heavy with blooms.
Inside a neatly swept barrack, sunlight warms the floors.
There is a barbed wire fence and a stilted guard tower—
But they are reminders, decorations, props with no power.

I stand eighty years away from those first "camp" days.
In the tale of Urashima Tarō, *a young fisherman saves a turtle from the cruelty of children.*
Time is running out; soon, this camp will no longer exist in living memory.
Grateful for his help, the turtle tows Urashima down deep below the waves.
Already it feels like a ghost town, where bare-boned buildings make past lives into relics.
Among the coral is an exquisite palace filled with wonders, and a lovely princess.
Slurs carved in the barrack walls by the white workers who built them whisper antique hate.
Urashima passes three days in bliss before remembering his elderly parents above.
Reviving this place feels like a task worthy of mythology, or twisted

fable.

Go, says the princess, and take this tamatebako, *this gift, to remember me; but do not open it!*

I am bound to try, but I know how much of what was here will never be recalled.

Urashima eagerly swims to the surface, clutching the black lacquered box.

The sky is an empty bowl. There are endless open fields, and the mountain.

He wades heavily to shore, weighed down by wet clothes.

Each breeze slips through my ribs like wind whistling through warped barrack walls.

The path looks different. His boat is gone. He hurries for home.

I imagine how it was before—no fields, no flowers, no warmth, nothing fresh or green.

A strange house is on the spot where home was. Urashima scratches his head.

Only dust and shame were shared in spades.

What are you looking for? an old man asks. My home, Urashima says. It was here when I left.

There was no indignity too small, no suffering too great. They defy calculation.

He gives his name. The old man laughs. Urashima Tarō disappeared centuries ago!

I long to list every ache and pain, to taxonomize them neatly and balance each.

But I am Urashima, the young man says.

But I might sooner count every head of wheat below the mountain.

Well, I don't know where you have been, says the old man, but you have been gone a long time.

Most survivors took their pain with them. There are burdens that were never set down.

What passed as three days for Urashima below the waves was three centuries above them.

After a year passed in camp, the *nikkei* farmers raised a bumper crop from barren desert.

Alone by the water, Urashima tugs on the silken cord, and lifts the lid of the black tamatebako.

They had to build two cellars to hold it all. (The empty earthen cellars are still here.)

Three plumes of purple smoke emerge, adding three centuries to his life.

They planted flowers, only to leave when they were in bloom. But the beauty remains.

In the next compartment, Urashima finds a mirror. An old man looks back at him.

How can I be filled with so much pride in such a place? My eyes overflow.

The waves roll in. Urashima dies. The sea princess weeps, knowing her love did not obey her.

I can't speak Japanese. The stories I was raised on are watercolor translations.

Alone by the water, Urashima tugs on the silken cord, and lifts the lid of the black tamatebako.

As an adult, I find the translations often sweetened the tales; made them softer.

Three plumes of purple smoke emerge, adding three centuries to his life.

I wonder what I miss in these translations. I wonder if I am missing something essential.

In the next compartment, Urashima finds a mirror. An old man looks back at him.

But standing here, surrounded by others like me, I find that I am more than myself.

The waves roll in. Urashima opens the final compartment. A feather drifts out.

The wind rises. I hold myself, pressing my hands against my heart before the mountain.

The feather touches him, light as a kiss, and turns him into a crane.

The suffering and the joy and the shame are all mine; unearned, but inherited.

He soars above the waves, forever in this world but apart from it.

I polish these heirlooms, wear them, wait for the day where I know how to display them.

He can no longer swim below the tide, in the quiet world of water,

The breeze carries the scent of sun-warm fennel. I feel the weight of what was lost.

But he can see more from here, and he is flying.

But it is enough to stand here under the clouds, my heart filled with
every breath of wind.

Terry Watada

●●●●●●●●●●

Summer Stars

for Midori Iwasaki
2022: To commemorate the 80th anniversary of the internment

Light from
over-
    head stars
  trickles
            down &
coats the glistening
barbed wire in the
muted
    summer
  night

in the woods
that have been
silent   for a 1000 years

canadian   prisoners
bleed
            memories of
    the lost
    streets, laughter and
    rain of Japanese Vancouver,

    the waterfront—distant
    breezes
    whispers of times past

a lump
in the throat, an ache
in the body.

the stars
shine brightly
above
Petawawa
concentration camp
un-
aware of pain
& loss.

and I feel the prickly heat
of the summer beneath
those
very same stars (

80 years later)

it scrapes across my skin
like
barbed wire.

it heats the blood
with
the sting of
injustice

it squeezes the eyes
with
tears of humidity
and the salt of hatred.

Summer stars:

the woods
        silently
absorb the light.

the trees
hold
    their prisoners,
reduced to their
elements in

the Precambrian
shield   a land-
scape of
    anonymous
  dead.

below the stars,
the empty and invisible
            still whisper
of their loss
of
    home and
 kin

as they strain to pull on the haunted
and blank
faces
    of ghosts
    & spirits.

Michael Prior

• • • • • • • • • •

Tashme

Taylor, Shirras, Mead

At ten, I thought it sounded Japanese—
the name no name but acronym, initials.
Older, visiting in winter, needles
fall from the pines like chaff's steel-
storm across my face.

Is this the signal or its foil?
That I thought the name was Japanese.
The valley channels what's left of a coastal breeze
scattering deadfall's initials
across what snow's erased.

Lines Written While Visiting the Valley Where the Camp Was

It happened here. RVs and summer homes.
    Salal clotting by the river.
A pair of black lungs' rotting petals
    on the back of a pack of Belmont Milds
half-buried in the reeds. If I try,
    I can crack the highway's asphalt,
lift it east across the valley, where it was
    when tarpaper shacks once rose
like mushrooms from the mud
    along the water—then deeper,
straighter, raked by winter wind
    into heaps of etched glass,
broken lines in which I might find
    a pair of sunken eyes, the grooves
of a forehead, slope of a nose,
    my grandmother leaning close
to crease a sheet of washi into a heart,
    a crane, a little frog; the little whisky
on my grandfather's breath the time
    he showed me how to swing a bat,
the way its momentum should point
    past home; or my mother
sobbing on the phone after I left mine in anger
    at nineteen. Like water
carried in cupped hands, all this was gone
    before I noticed. It persists
as motion rehearsed into muscle.
    I'm alone and tired of trying
to summon years from the valley's blue-green
    shadows, the white-tailed deer
silent as sentries among the trees.
    Dear grandparents, dear parents, dear

derelict feeling: whose beginning
    is written on the plaque outside
the visitor's center? Which futures
    still flicker like the embers
    constellating the end
of a half-extinguished cigarette?

Garrett Kurai

•••••••••

The Return

Our buses circle like wagons
as the wind blows Manzanar sand
into our Kentucky Fried Chicken.
Being the youngest, they choose me
to pick out raffle tickets.
Peeking through my father's fingers,
I cull the name of my grandmother
for a prize of toilet paper.

The wind dies as we retrace the forgotten
barracks and barbed wires reminding
us that *good fences make good neighbors.*
All I find in the dust is a golden bullet shell.

Some twenty years later I return,
sliding down from a wedding in Independence.
We plop out of a rented van
into the July heat. This time,
I notice the stone shells of buildings
like mussels that won't let go.
All that remains of suffering are shells.
Maybe, if I put one to my ear,
I can hear a hell of yesteryear.

Brandon Shimoda

• • • • • • • • • • • • •

Gila River

The prisoners lived for many years—
had children   grandchildren great-grandchildren

burned very quietly
to ash,

cut rectangles in the floor   dug holes in the dirt
to stay cool
in July   folded their bodies
like paper   fell asleep
in the holes   rivers evaporated. The prisoners disintegrated
Not even their secrets

Japanese Americans were not looking at themselves
turning white
not the cotton   not the descendants of bloodless cotton
the children's fathers refused to pick

Children were shy   had stories to tell,
not their own, but those not resolved, still dirty

a nisei woman was asked if she would like to speak, share her story
the people   facing the gleaming snow
looked sad, for a moment,   then vulturous. sad again

expectant, ready to ascend.

The nisei woman shook her head,   No, she said.
Are you sure, she was asked.
I don't remember enough
to share   She said
As she was looking through the snow   She remembered everything
but could not, seven decades later, associate herself with the subjects,
by whom her memory was reminded.

When the children arrived, there were turtles Snapping turtles
like helmets   greeted the children
Turtles deep
deep deep
in the ditches, slowly rose   and snapped at the children
like Yoshiko,   wearing a dress   of her mother's crumpled face,
walked right up to the ditch
and peered in:

children were grabbed, pulled in, became turtles

How could she forget
the turtles were the solace of America

You don't forget   You are tricked,
into putting your hand in
mirror-green water. Your hand stays stuck

you stop looking

eyes were olives. Children were torches

One of each twin drowned
or burned down

to the dirt
where grandparents   on their hands and knees
re-enacted the rose, the thorn

Long hair dangled
over water   seasons stretched
camouflage nets
across the suburbs. shotgun shells   spoons, heels of shoes,
talons, forked tongues, arrow-tipped tails,
the wake of a temple
men sitting beneath spiraling flowers

mother was very popular
with the ghosts
that grew out of the ditches   they were soldiers
deep into the harmony of their hunger

Children sat on the hill
watched the desert changing colors   the stars
lower
on tendons

movies smelled   Carcasses came out

to narrate the silences

some sank into the cold, impenetrable shrapnel
fallen from tens of thousands of miles

only children remember to forget
with such warm innocence   being struck
by the sun
not innocence Guilt

not the opposite of innocence   But
like the dissolution of a flower into fruit,
compensation
and the will to be stolen

Noriyuki was eleven, had spinal TB
when he was incarcerated as an enemy of the United States   His body
    was cut
from the cast   and propped up
in front of the moving mirage   Noriyuki,
better
or worse known as
Mr. Miyagi, for whom Noriyuki put on the accent
of an immigrant from Okinawa

His inscrutability was part of the trick   the coming into consciousness
of a Japanese man
who had no one   war extinguished
Truth,   the FBI trained him
to be someone else,   not other, but native
by pretending to be someone else,   not native, but foreign

He stood in the bush
until the bush became ice

When Mr. Miyagi gets drunk   and relives the war
are we not supposed to imagine Noriyuki, the actor,
summoning the memory
of the war he was living
as a child   prisoner

is that misunderstanding
or a misunderstanding

Did you have anyone in the 442nd

No, I said,   My ancestors are not corpses
propped upright in the corner
My ancestors do not stand in cold rooms in the dark   draped with lights
round cancerous   in which my face is warped   waiting
to be turned on   dance in the window

From afar   incarceration looks like internment
It is always day
No   Japanese Americans exist
at night   The river is full   Japanese Americans gather
in the sundown   on the banks of the abundant river
to pay respects
to the primal thinking
of white men and women,   distant, futuristic
summer   or winter
or walking down the reservation

wild animals raised their heads   land stretched away
The further away from the train
the less it moved

children watched their parents' faces
framed in squares
and rectangles of light   seam of stars,
then dark,
then darkness

Did it feel like travel? guarantee of returning?
Their movements were curtailed. sound was rhythmic suture.
Dreams of the wheels slipping off

wild animals moved fast. in the shadows of rocks:

I will see you
again. incriminated

by the sadness
of someone else's dream

without ending   migration becomes internal
for those who do not leave
keep the memory leaving

de-located,   graves doubled

migration was a test. the destination was the extent to which
a soul could be transformed. The United States wanted to replace
with a clock,

the furnace of assimilation. earth harbors
unintelligible tongues
in the core,   tongues of flame, they are called,
the earth answers
with its cavernous body, I release you
into the custody of culture   Enslaving, exploiting,
exterminating   takes its toll   The toll is paid
by the enslaved,
exploited, exterminated

How did it feel to be surrounded by Japanese Americans
with whom you were not related?   Prison
is prolongation   I felt like
I was standing in
a graveyard   waiting for the sun
to pass into eclipse   for the light to christen
what was buried beneath
the long, ship-like passage of shadow

I don't remember the way you remember
I don't remember a prison, but Easter
I don't remember which season or burying

In the forbidden sight
of each blackened window
a face permeated

the face of each
age of death.

fit fruitfully into
a box.   Each face was made   Each face made real
pores that recalled
the frustrated youth of grandmothers.

Why is your skin so smooth, my grandmother asked
one night. I came out of the bathroom. I was a child.
The night was supposed to feel endless, insatiable,
was stunted   I saw myself in the window   superimposed
on a tree,   and a deer, with red eyes
cut in half

I wash my face, I said
I wash my face too

Kenneth Tanemura

• • • • • • • • • • • • • •

Former Site of an Internment Camp

Is not blue, is not the color of oak,
we all looked at and through it and with it
and saw very little of it, wondered what it was,
if it would transform into form, survive
a forensic examination, require more of us
than the us who were there then, who were strained
to imagine the barbed wire fence not-there,
the one that went missing, and it showed
there was nothing there anymore
if there ever had been, if there ever existed
a trace of the truth about the place
where we came to find, if in the fence
facing east once one guessed it was a house
in a forest or a tree, the coveted tree house
of back then, where one could live with the leaves,
leave when one wanted, could want anything
up around the branches that desired everything
and nothing is what was seen
after all that had fallen into place

Leanne Toshiko Simpson

tankas for a buried town

i.

wounds of lost train tracks
burnt into indifferent green –
here, fall into the
yawning mouth of a lake that
holds ancestors lost to grief

ii.

climb the fence between
white bodies and ours, observe
the cedar post that
stands for us – *seirei to* – in
a town afraid to forget

iii.

find arteries of
survival in the tofu
factory, ice rink
turned mess hall – Canadian
hospitality in bloom

iv.

we are your stories,
whistling through scant cracks in these

hakujin houses
built with the stripped lumber of
our family's second exile

v.

when we step into
the only diner for miles,
they know why we have
come, and we know we'll never
find the words we're looking for

Aisuke Kondo

●●●●●●●●●●

with English translations by Kondo and Yukiko Nagakura

石

収容されたあなたは

ここで毎日何かを思い

そしてあなたの記憶は散りばめられ

その記憶は石になる

この場所に収容された全ての人々の記憶も

散りばめられ

その記憶は石になり

あなたの石と

あなたではない石が混ざり

私は一つ一つの石に尋ね

あなたを拾う

Stones

You were incarcerated here

You thought of something every day here

Your memories were scattered here

Your memories turned into stones here

People were incarcerated here

Their memories were also scattered here

Their memories turned into stones here

Your stones and others's stones were mixed here

I ask each stone here

I pick up the pieces of your memories here

トパーズ

72年前

あなたはこの場所に収容され

あなたは自由を奪われ

あなたは先住民の石鏃を拾う

72年後

あなたの居たこの場所で

あなたが日本へ持ち帰った石鏃を

私は手の中に握りしめ

あなたに会う

あなたが置き忘れた魂の半分に

Topaz

72 years ago

You were incarcerated in this place

You were deprived of your freedom

And you picked up a stone arrowhead from indigenous people

72 years later

In this place where you were

I stand

Here

In my hands

The stone arrowhead you brought back to Japan

I meet you

The half of your soul, you left here

山

私はあなたの身体が収容されていたこの場所に立つ

私はあなたのアイデンティティが収容されていたこの場所に立つ

私はあなたの感情が収容されていたこの場所に立つ

私はあなたの記憶が収容されていたこの場所に立つ

私はあなたの魂が収容されていたこの場所に立つ

そして私はこの場所でのあなたの生活を想像し

そして私はふと気づく

私を見下ろすその存在に

私を囲むその存在に

山

山はまるで壁のように

山は私を見ていて

山は私を監視していた

山はあなたをいつも見ていて

山はあなたをいつも監視していた

山は彼・彼女らをいつも見ていて

山は彼・彼女らをいつも監視していた

私は絵を描いた

私は線を引いた

かつてあなたが描いたかもしれない

あの山を描いた

Mountains

I stand in this place where your body was incarcerated

I stand in this place where your identity was incarcerated

I stand in this place where your emotions were incarcerated

I stand in this place where your memories were incarcerated

I stand in this place where your soul was incarcerated

Imagine your life in this place

I suddenly realize

There is something standing like a wall

There is something surrounding me

Mountains

Like a wall

Mountains watch me

Mountains monitor me

They look down on me

They surround me

Mountains

Mountains always watched you

Mountains always monitored you

Mountains always watched them

Mountains always monitored them

I drew a picture

I drew the lines

Once you might have drawn

I drew those mountains

Doug Yamamoto

●●●●●●●●●●●●

At Manzanar the Mountains

The sun covers snow
Covered mountain peaks with
Lean brilliant light

You stab dust
In blind battles

Sierra granite
Mesquite, jack rabbits
Wind through dead orchards
Cow dung, sage
Broken concrete

More than reasons
To be here

Barracks vanished
To the backcountry
Of an issei woman's
Closed eyes

Purple irises
Packed in spring snow
Bloom in tin cans
Under the Manzanar
Monument

Sand

That got past tar paper
That flew by pine boards and curtains
And washed into dry gullies
Soaks up teardrops
Clear salty wings

A song shakes loose
From the earth
A shakuhachi body
A melody
Rides high on the wires
Whistling Lone Pine winds
Across the storm worn valley

Tall Sierra Nevada.
Barbed wire
Shreds the wind.
Tombstone sound
Of guntowers.

On the corner
This block of
Right where we live

Claire Kageyama-Ramakrishnan

Shadow Mountain

1. Gift Without Purchase

This is for the child's awed gaze,
his fear of the landscape's vast alluviums,
for the dry lids and tears no cool cloth
swabs, for the rub and chill of ground
sediments, ash and sand, allergens—
mice dandruff and droppings, this is for
his attempt to breathe air, saccular
spasms inside his impenetrable chest,
this is for nightmares inside him, phlegm
plugging airways, his feverish forehead,
for the child's inflammatory response,
(the one you can't see) inside the branches
and whorls of his psyche, for the array
of pain in his trachea and stomach,
for the inexplicable rhythm coursing
below clavicle and sternum,
auricular, ventricular tunnels,
for spirals the microscope misses,
molecules between his heart, mind,
and spirit. This is for the grown child,
the beat of defeat he never explains.

2. First Trip to Manzanar

When I stepped out of the car and stood *there*—
before the vertical and angular pillar,
smaller than the Washington Monument, white
with strokes of Japanese calligraphy,

when someone pointed and said, *Your father lived here,*
when I saw the trace of the block's rectangle,
when I stepped over the flaked remains of obsidian,
ants as large as my fingernails, when my uncle aimed
his camera at us, when my father tightened and said nothing,
when my sister dropped a Crush can inside
our temporary trash carrier—empty Cheetos bag,
when my brother said he really had *to go*
and my mother told him to wait
for the bathroom in the next town—*Independence,*
when my father reached and lit a new cigarette,
said he was through, he was ready to leave,
when I sat in the front seat with my mother
and my father drove around for one last look,
slowed to see a black Chevrolet, beat, antiqued
by a spray of bullets on the driver's side,
corrosion and rust devouring each hole,
when I eyed the mountains shadowed violet
in the distance, the rumble of thunder shook us,
turned us inward as my father drove North,
when my sister kneeled on the backseat
to wave at my brother and uncle following us,
the rain fell in big drops and the spattered insects
stayed stuck to each window, I choked on spit,
knew, without knowing how to tie my shoelaces,
the air was angry, the shadows followed us,
the spirits inside the camp weren't resting

3. Photograph of My Grandmother: Outside a Desert Chapel, After her Release from Patton State Hospital

There are the half-lit thoughts,
the flash without the coveted negatives.
Where was his mother? What did
the interrogators ask his father in Santa Fe?
A cloth spine bent with conclusions.
If thoughts privilege the consequence
of imagining, is there a limit to what we imagine,

to fallacies if we rely on the sublime?
Writing without the sublime—Is that
even possible? The luxuries of scribbles
without censorship. Uncertainties are the antithesis
of proofs. Security, a gain of the absolute.
The mark of equations: solids turned to vapor,
ice evaporating into air, moisture
rimming the lip and exterior of a glass,
chilled drink's loss of upward
bubbles. Numbers and formulas map
the liquid's properties. They cannot explain
a child's dream of petroglyphs,
the photographer's words on the back
of a photograph: *Not to be Reproduced, Ansel Adams.*
My uncle paid one dollar. His reason:
to fill one page of our album. The reprint,
record of lost hours, proof
his mother smiled, relied on prayer, a priest
to intervene. The reprint, trace
of violations before the shutter snapped.

4. Form Breaks: Late Night Apostrophe
Chilled by the sting of wind and vertigo,
he spies clouds half-shadowing the mountains
like paradise after the first biblical fall.
This is what he wonders: did the nights get this dull
in the Garden? Will his parents return as ash?
How long does the stab of one long eyelash last?
Will the pain in his eye from the stiff lash
stop? Did Adam's ears ache with vertigo?
Nothing is absolute, not even the ash
scatterings of truth ground in the mountains.
The pain is difficult to isolate this dull
night of apostrophe. His questions fall
in ripe clusters with midnight's steady fall
of diagonal rain stirring the last
words to settle the confusion and dull

the anxious spell of vertigo.
Here I write,
                                        Wind upturns dust. The mountain's
architecture shifts. Faultlines fill with ash.
Ground's layers can't hold. The self survives its ash.
Earth's plates break. Gravity pulls a fall—
out of snow on plush mountains.

How long did his first winter in Camp last?
Where did he play tic-tac-toe and *Go*,
learn to genuflect, steer clear of dulled
barbed wire scraps, the guards cradling their dull
arms. Wild Wind, help me gather up the ash,
the lives fraught with fear and vertigo.
Dust the photographs of the first fall
shots snapped by the camera's lens, the last
black and white stills of deserted mountains,
the snow-capped points of Sierra mountains,
spare the branches of the apple tree, dull
and gray with age. Wild Wind, blow in the last
gesture to protest the interned, their ash
black, wide eyes in photographs, the first Fall
shots to hide my father's fever and vertigo.
                                                                                Write with me,

Wind upturns   dust.   The mountain's
architecture shifts.   Fault lines fill with ash.
Ground's   layers   can't hold. The self
survives   its ash.   Earth's plates break.

Gravity spins a fall—
out of tense shifts.
                                        Form breaks from the mountains.

Find the photograph—
                                                    the apple tree, frail
and pale with age,
the faces of disguised rage

5. Terzanelle: Manzanar Riot

This is a poem with missing details,
of ground gouging each barrack's windowpane,
sand crystals falling with powder and shale,

where silence and shame make adults insane.
This is about a midnight of searchlights,
of ground gouging each barrack's windowpane,

of syrup on rice and a cook's big fight.
This is the night of Manzanar's riot.
This is about a midnight of searchlights,

a swift moon and a voice shouting, Quiet!
where the revolving searchlight is the moon.
This is the night of Manzanar's riot,

windstorm of people, rifle powder fumes,
children wiping their eyes clean of debris,
where the revolving searchlight is the moon,

and children line still to use the latrines.
This is a poem with missing details,
children wiping their eyes clean of debris—
sand crystals falling with powder and shale.

6. One Question, Several Answers

Where did your father live?
    House on Federal, City of Angels.

Where did your father live?
    Horse stall at a racetrack.

Where did your father live?
    Near the aqueduct, in a man-made desert.

Where did your father live?

By a pear tree.
With pears, ripe pears from that tree.

Where did your father live?
Block 25.

Where did your father live?
With thin strips of tarpaper.
Pot under his straw mattress.

Where did your father live?
Waiting in line to use the latrines.
Waiting in line at the mess hall.
Waiting for his parents.

Where did your father live?
The Desert Chapel.

Where did your father live?
With his brothers,
transplants—Joshua trees.

Where did your father live?
In his mother's heart.

Where did your father live?
Barrack 12, Unit 3.

Where did your father live?
With 5 strand barbs.
With windstorms and bitterbrush.
With years of snowmelt, glacial erasure.

7. Death at Manzanar, 1943
Did anyone tell you
he walked barefoot through ticks?

He filled ground holes with marbles.
He touched the South side fence
when the guards weren't looking.

He heard coyotes upset the chickens,
saw veins spread over the desert.

He liked pears more than apples.
His favorite color was blue.
He liked high places.

Did anyone tell you
he reached for an apple?

Poison spread through his ankle.
He never felt the bite
or heard the rattle.

Did anyone tell you
he loved Pleasure Park,

the bridge over the stream?
He kept a bird-tip arrowhead.
He was an orphan at the Children's Village.

He thought Heaven lurked behind,
in the shade of a mountain.

He thought he'd see

his mother and father again.
He thought he'd say good-bye
to everyone in camp.

He believed Heaven a place
without barbed wire.

8. Reasons Without Answers: Visiting the Ruins of a Japanese Internment Camp in Northern California

Someday when someone tells me reasons why
　　my parents make me stand so still right here,
I'll exhale deep breaths of relief to know
　　their silence in snapping these photographs
of the rock and pagoda-roofed guard house,
　　where there's something my father can still see,

feel deeply for a past I cannot see,
　　save a few fragments when I wonder why
they look here for the flimsy, invisible house,
　　a dirt spread, a block that hasn't been here
so many years, except in photographs
　　Ansel Adams took and developed; he knew

what most people didn't want to know,
　　the truth they tried so hard not to see.
They burned his pamphlet of photographs,
　　photos I'll find and ask my uncle why
this happened, could this happen again here?
　　I'll turn the worn pages to find the house

thin walled and tar-papered, unlike the house
　　I live in hearing parents say, *No,*
you can't be a Brownie or Girl Scout here,
　　you can't go to Summer Camp, can't you see
these people might be bad, that's why
　　you can't, as I study the photographs

of Manzanar, the only photograph
　　I'll have of the block with my father's house
I'll copy for ten cents, wondering why
　　my uncle tells me, *Never say what you know,*
and I won't ask my father what he sees
　　when he relives life again here,

the volcanic ash, sage, obsidian here,
    the wind howling when they snap photographs,
my father's mounting tension when he sees
    That Shithead Roosevelt in the guard house,
a survivor's rage to let the world know
    there are reasons why, good reasons why

the words remain inside the guard house,
    parents drive here to take photographs,
their children wonder, they can't tell them why.

9. Mountain and Shadow
I don't know what happened next.

> *The bus arrived. They entered the desert.*
> *The youngest son cried for his missing parents,*
> *then stopped.*

> R

Manzanar

> *Spanish for Apple Orchard.*
> *A metonym for taking fathers and sons,*
> *place that locked grandmothers up.*

In Japanese

> *"kage" means "shadow,"*
>
> *"yama" is "mountain."*

How will you write the camp?

> *With a lowercase and capital "C."*

With the fear of disappointing you and them.

In a dream I am reunited
with a view of Mount Williamson.
My brother, sister, and I are at Manzanar.

We're on our way to Independence,
the town after the camp.
I am standing and waiting

at the first guard house, my hands folded,
as if I am waiting to receive the Sacraments,
waiting for Baptism and Communion,

waiting for the Father, the Son, and the Spirit—
for the gift of flames or tongues.
Before flesh parted with spirit,

our grandparents and relatives were here…
Suddenly, my niece and nephew appear.
I say our relatives' bodies aren't buried

below the cemetery marker
with Japanese calligraphy,
but their spirits reside here.

Whatever is left of this camp,
my niece, my nephew,
is your legacy.

Your grandfather lived here.
Every year in the middle of summer,
I stood here with your father and aunt.

II

This Is Not the Whole Story

● ● ● ● ● ● ● ● ● ●

This is not the whole story,
and yet, it is true.
It is a story without an ending.
And when I open my mouth
to speak, it continues.

—**Christine Kitano,**
"1942: In Response to Executive Order 9066,
My Father, Sixteen, Takes"

W. Todd Kaneko

• • • • • • • • • • •

Legacies of Camp

1.
The first rule in talking about camp is
we do not talk about camp.

2.
Minidoka is a word we use for camp.
Relocation is a fancy way of talking
about internment, camp a polite
word for prison. Minidoka.

3.
The cage is the skeleton for grief, grief
the mantle worn by shame, shame the fuel
for a tone-deaf heart.

4.
They say this is where the witch burned,
where the ogre lost his heart. Sing a real song
for imaginary creatures. Keep it simple
so the ghosts can sing along.

5.
Men bruised by sticks.
Men pummeled by stones.
Men disintegrated by wind.
Men gashed to pieces by wild animals.
Men shredded by flights of dark birds.
Men evaporating into morning.

6.
What turns kings into beasts, princesses
into crones hungry for dusk? How do we lose
our ancestors still living in barren houses
next door? What do horses dream about,
buttressed by the rigor mortis of night?
Remember: we do not talk about camp.

7.
The second rule: There are no trick questions,
only bear traps poised silent in hope
that someone will talk about camp.

8.
The cage houses the heart of the ogre,
the ogre the glamor bewitching
the wilderness. We live at the fringe
of awful desire, that ragged edge of twilight
where the ocean devours the shore.
Remember the cage.

9.
They say those ruins are nearly swallowed
by the Idaho scrubland. I've seen ruins
posing as old men on bar stools, women
cloaked in thorns and sharks' teeth.
We do not talk about ruins.

10.
Men who smoke in restaurants.
Men who try to quit smoking.
Men who try to quit smoking for their children.
Men who smoke only when drinking.
Men who smoke in cars with the windows up.
Men who smoke in secret places.
Men who never knew they were on fire.

11.
The cage shelters us from despair, despair
the ocean lapping at our knees, fear the eels
wriggling electric on the incoming tide.
The cage holds everything we do not talk about.

12.
Third rule: Do not speak—listen to buzzards
pasted against every sunset, to alley cats
yowling lonesome in the glow of night.
That is a soliloquy of ruin. This is
the hush of mushrooms on fallen trees.

13.
Stories are tiny prisons built to house
our secrets. We live in cages still.
My grandmother's legs remain bound
by barbed wire. My grandfather's tongue
lay caked in dust. Everyone is dead.
It was goddamn camp—we can't talk about it.

shō yamagushiku

•••••••••••••

[the ocean and i]

"No person of Japanese origin was ever convicted of any acts of espionage during the Second World War."

the ocean and i   what a seditious pair

on foggy san pedro mornings
we tap the currents

tracing tendons

we master the day's

telegram before it breaks, a

handwhisper

to that root ancestor on backhome island

we speak the minutiae of military installations
of roving ivory currents rushing whales home
and how to grenade a language

and ride
a pelican's wings so they do not tire,

the journey long
long

in climes of boredom
me and my comrades pick up urchins

                                        hurl them like counterfeit atomic bombs
                                        into this stillborn country

muddied water rushing a
revolutionary's conscience

grabbing at an ethic, then
losing it to the storm

where came winter's immortalized
destruction, roosevelt's men carving
my watery wrists, tendons exposing
a guerrilla offensive, a people marked

             hanging in the
                          winds of those prolific camps

                          swinging
                                        and swinging

                          the spring sun curing me into
                          jerky for long evacuations
                          lanky men languishing and
                          lancing into me

                          me, sticking in their yellow teeth
                          me, caked in stomach acid
                          me, looking into the blacks
                          of their eyes a fountain

of sequins, aquamarine moments
that must be held together to
betray our salacious secrets

the henchman
horrified
then hard

for how much i knew

(san pedro, 1941)

Mia Ayumi Malhotra

●●●●●●●●●●●●●●

A History of Isako

I.

During war Isako is lady watch city fade to rubble. Is lady hide in Kobe church as air raid siren shrill overhead. Is lady strain for voice of emperor on radio then sell kimono and shred boiled potato to rice. Is lady watch as shrapnel slice body like pickled ginger to be dyed pink and buried. Dip finger in saltwater then take rice in cupped palm. Press tightly and release. Is lady cross Pacific on S.S. Cleveland. Isako is lady turn from train track when spat upon. Is lady in Arkansas desert. Is lady wipe dust from tin plate in mess hall. Is released from camp to board Whites Only train. Is lady wipe spittle from cheek in Cincinnati and leave sorority. Mark difference. Isako is lady tape name to bottom of casserole dish before church potluck. Tuck blade beneath box spring next to No. 11 knitting needle. Behind barbed wire all question run to one.

II.

I do not remember where Isako is during the war. Is it Osaka or Ohio. I do not wish to appear foolish. There is the question of authenticity.

When I write about Isako I use words like _________ and _________ knowing such designations make no sense. I use these details to make Isako at home on a page that is otherwise white.

I put the rim of my teacup against my lip and blow to create a dampening effect.

I wish to write about this important person in my life but cannot do so without saying ________ or ________.

Instead I write about dust. A pigment that stains yellow and cannot be removed.

III.

I wear a kimono only once in my life. The garment once belonged to Isako although it has been hemmed twice and bears several discolorations on the bodice. I have no idea how to reassemble the garment and leave it poorly folded in its paper sleeve. Traditionally this knowledge is passed from mother to daughter. Isako scolds me for rumpling the collar then smoothes it along the traditional folds. A kimono tied right over left is a sign that the wearer is deceased. In English all words begin in the left margin and disappear into the right. I rewrap the garment believing a new grammar may be necessary.

IV.

instructions to all living persons Japanese in the following ancestry area persons alien will be evacuated pursuant to from non-alien ancestry noon provisions this dated 12 o'clock P.W.T. Saturday Commanding Executive Order No. 34 no persons will be permitted living no Japanese will be living to change residence area after 12 o'clock noon P.W.T. Saturday May 9, 1942 without obtaining permission the Commanding General Civil Control Station located permits will be granted such only for purpose the uniting members or family emergency grave in cases evacuees must carry property following them on departure for Assembly Center between hours the 8AM the 5PM bedding (no mattress) linens for members each of family articles toilet for members each of family will be packaged marked plainly with name and owner numbered in accordance

Tamiko Nimura

• • • • • • • • • • •

Instructions to All Persons of Japanese Ancestry (an erasure)

for my Yonsei daughters

Uniting members of a family
to assist, give,
provide respect to all,

the following instructions must be observed:
(A responsible name is held,
living,
to receive further instructions.)

Evacuees carry with them the following:
Family, extra family,
sufficient family,
essential personal family.

All will be securely tied, plainly marked.
That which can be carried by the individual or family group will be permitted.
The substantial will be accepted.

All instructions pertaining to the movement will be obtained.
Go to 1942 to receive further instructions.

Kurt Yokoyama Ikeda

•••••••••••••••

"Only what you can carry"

Inspired by "De donde soy yo" by Levi Romero and with permission from George Ella Lyon of "Where I'm from." Process your pilgrimage through poetry. Fill in the blanks with memories and community.

Where are you from?
________________ (A place where you call home)
No really, where are you from?

I am from ________________ (the weather around where you live)
The ________________ (plant or tree near your home)
"Whose long gone limbs I remember as if they were my own".

Only ________________ (object passed down from a family member)
What ________________ (family members), left for me, remembers that.
You Can Carry Home.

I carry ________________ (an everyday item in your home) and ________________ (everyday item in your home)
From the ________________ (description of your home)
I carry ____________ (family food), ____________ (family food), and ____________ (kitchen utensils or condiments)
On ________________ (a holiday, a season, or a celebration) also.
I carry ________________ (a song, song lyric, or a dance) on ________________ (day of the week or season)
I carry ___________ (something you were told as a child) and ___________ (another thing you were told as a child)

Only ________________ (someone you have lost) and
________________ (someone else you have lost)
Who are now memories, know that
You can carry ________________ (your choice), where I'm from.

I carry ________________ (place of birth) and
________________ (other places you call home)
I carry ________________ (important people in your life)
And ________________ (an important date) too.
I carry ________________ (family names)
I carry ________________ (places that are important to your family)
I pilgrimage to you.

From ________________ (write about a family member who has passed)
To ________________ (write about a family member who is living)
I carry ________________ (the emotion you feel about these people)
Only what you can't ______________ (see/feel/hear) is
______________ (something your family left behind or lost)
I carry this in my heart
So, when you ask me, where I am from.
Know that I carry ________________ (your choice)

Now, where are you from?

Michael Prior

●●●●●●●●●

A Hundred and Fifty Pounds

Each adult will be allowed 150 pounds
and each child will be allowed 75 pounds of baggage.
—B.C. Security Commission, 1942

after Kayla Isomura's The Suitcase Project

In some, the luggage lies open
like a mouth mid-sentence.
In others, closed zippers grimace:

What would you have brought?
Slippers, a stuffed platypus, a gold watch
on a chain, copper pots swaddled in bedding.

The hypotheses: that thinking
can be things, that each decision shrinks
the pained mind to the space

inside a suitcase. Include
lacquered chopsticks, silver forks,
a hammer scarred by rust, the orders

nailed to telephone poles and doors.
Omit what you whispered then,
most of what you've seen.

I was given forty-eight hours' notice, twenty-four.
I passed ice and pines and plains.

I rode an iron serpent

into the Interior
beside four hundred others.
It was humid. It was cold.

If pain is remembered
to be dismissed. If fear still seeds
its rotting forest. This

is a gardener's trowel, a blue skein of yarn,
a violin, a ukulele, a ukulele, a ukulele.
This is a porch light

flicked on and off in abscessed night.
These are pear blossoms falling
on the driveway like footprints in black ice.

Memories, river stones,
metamorphic and worn. How many
might an able-bodied individual carry

through livestock-stalls and mud,
onto a bus, a train,
into a tiny, uninsulated shack?

Most say the same: *It could happen again.*
It is happening now, I couldn't
make room

for a dogless collar,
a hound's-tooth scarf, a steel urn
packed in Styrofoam, a letter

recording blood's divisive fractions.
My father would not have come.
My mother. My stepsister. My brother.

What matters is not what you bring,
but what you keep.
She was there. He was, too.

Christine Kitano

●●●●●●●●●●●

1942: In Response to Executive Order 9066, My Father, Sixteen, Takes

No spare underwear.
No clean shirts, pants, or good shoes.
Instead, a suitcase
of records. His trombone.
This is not the whole story,
and yet, it is true.
It is a story without an ending.
And when I open my mouth
to speak, it continues.

Aaron Caycedo-Kimura

Dad Called It *Camp*

Tule Lake   Jerome Arkansas   the Santa Anita Racetrack
but to me as a boy   camp meant   a green pup tent
blue-and-white water jug   Coleman gas stove   packed
in the back   of our Ford Falcon wagon   Mom Dad Mari me
swaddled together   two sleeping bags   warm even in rain
Mari with tight grip   at each end   of a stick
gill-kebobbing   five silvery fish   Dad caught in the lake
he said he learned   to cook in camp   perfected judo throws
in brother Mits's club   chased brother Frank   with a garter snake
sounded like   a long vacation   *my mother got sick and died*
in camp   the only sad thing he said   no mention
of barbed wire   guard towers   cold wind or hot dust
blowing through rows   and rows   and rows of barracks

Brian Komei Dempster

Seized

By day. By night. In handcuffs. Through mind-scramble. Brain-
surged. Shock of force, body taut. Alerted. Taken.
Outside. Inside. Anytime. Any place. No words to explain. My
infant mother, 1942. My young son now. The rug,
his twisted body, his world inside. And what it does. Red flare
or white lightning. Fried impulse or smoldering
heat. A searing of gray or glitter of stars veiled by fog. Her
fragments. Yellow orb, the porch light. Shimmer
against her face. The cradle, her mother's arms. A blanket's false
cover. Itch of wool, hives on skin. Things
just happen. By bus. By train. In war. Electric storms. A horse
stable. Desert. Sand swirl and mind gust. Thought
sparks. Word cloudings. Mountains spike against white. A guard's
boot. Trodden syllable. A thorned cage. Wing

pierced. Baby hawk in wire. My barbed string of words. To capture

    him. Capture her. If he never speaks? I carry him. If

she cries for her father? Grandmother carries her. Some place. My

    mother carries what is unremembered. Begins to know

when I ask. I don't speak. Of things I can't know. Of despair about

    my son. We never know. Where we are going. Where

love will end us.

Carolyn Nakagawa

•••••••••••••••

Evacuation

Everything was lost then,
though we already had nothing.

There is a place in you no one can enter,
thoughts stranded at its edges. That's what I mean
by memory, this vacancy marked as love.

I tried to hold you, but you had to leave
again, still looking to be safer
than home. You had to leave
and find someplace simpler,
where I wouldn't follow.

It was for my benefit.
Why call a thing what it is
if you can forget it, live
outside of what you gave me.

I don't need anything

from you except stillness. Try to leave
me here. Try to leave for something
easy. Try to leave me behind.

Anne Yukie Watanabe

yes, 1942

the train stops in the desert &
everyone falls to their knees
to pray.

there was no bullet to the head, but there was

the mother	who bled to death
in a horse stable	the sick boy
in the infirmary	the loyalty questionnaire asking

28. *will you be loyal from your cage*
27. *will you die for us?*

there were the young men who said yes
& got blown up
to save some white Texans.
there were the people
who said no &
got beat up by the people
who thought we would all be saved
by saying *yes,*
yes I'll die for you.

Christine Kitano

•••••••••••

Gaman

It was night when the buses stopped.
It was too dark to see the road,

or if there was a road. So we waited.
We watched. We thought of back home,

how the orchards would swell with fruit,
how the trees would strain, then give way

under their ripe weight. The pockmarked
moon the face of an apple, pitted

with rot. But of course not. Someone
would intervene, would make of our absence

a profit. When we came, the boat, anchored
at San Francisco Bay, swayed for hours…

the gauntlet of uniformed men so intent
on finding cause to turn us away. And now

again, we wait. We watch. Our American children
press against us with their small backs.

Which gives us pause. For the sake of the children,
we'll teach them to forgive the fear of others,

the offenses. But what we don't anticipate

is how the dust of the desert will clot our throats,

how much fear will conspire to keep us silent.
And how our children will read this silence

as shame. However much we tried, we thought,
to demonstrate grace. When the buses stopped,

it was too dark to see the road. Or if there was a road.
It was night. And instead of speaking, we waited.

Instead of speaking, we watched.

Traise Yamamoto

At Heart Mountain, 1942

A picture comes and then goes: slow light, cheap sacking
over the windows. You remember mostly
a blankness, willing it, an emptiness
to hold pain, like the vacancy
of wide-open flatland. Whatever fills it,
a cow town, an oasis, a single man
wandering, does not change the fact of emptiness.
You remember lying there trying
not to hope because hope
is too far from what is possible, too much
like trying to imagine a next life. You understand
only that you are in this place, and someone
somewhere else, you don't know where, but
anywhere, is worrying about an empty
coffee tin, fingerprints on the glass, lost tickets
to a dance. And that's as far as understanding goes.
You watch your life from the outside: a shirt
hangs on a doorknob, a woman's shoes
wait under the bed. What is yours
is not your own, so you shut your heart.
You know that each day comes,
will come, and between one and the other what happens,
happens. But you feel,
when you lie on your back at night
watching the ceiling turn dark and it is very still,
that there is no future. That is how you live.

Syd Westley

•••••••••

How did the physical space of the camps contribute to your experiences?

it was so. barren it was so. empty it was so. lonely. i never understood how a space could feel so. lifeless it was a. nothing that went on for. ever and now to find out it was a. land with so much. life it was a land with no conception of. empty it was a land of. peoples and not. lonelies and i guess it makes a kind of. sense is there a way to leave a space without. footprints is there a way to leave a space without. soil moved and. taken and. left behind it was so empty. as in an act of. remembrance as in an act of. not forgetting and you know the land does not. forget and you know the land does not forget. that it was the ground a. people were moved out of only so another. people could be moved. into of course there is a. point to this the movement of. peoples creates. empties and what was my experience if not. empty

Kenneth Tanemura

•••••••••••••••

Gila

Act so that there is no use in a center,
no need of any kind of support
from a single party in this area.
Living out of a shoebox or is it
in a shoebox and out of a suitcase?

Except they stayed in one place and not many,
and not briefly, and they collected things even in the desert.
They are still alive today at night when the world turns around
in a sea breeze or in an ice bath.

Only what they could carry was a theme back then,
making the rounds, rounding out the literature on the subject,
then writing a book about it in a journal
for the next few months in a journal
in the library of the city.

In the thick of war in the thick of it
there were many people who had never seen the books
in their own home before or in a museum in a city
that they thought they would never visit again
because it had no idea that the world existed in its own time.

The center of the internment camp was a center with sides,
with two columns in front of each other in a circle
of four rows of four or more people each
with the same height as a group of six and a quarter to six.
There's a would-be author warming up some hot water for tea,

he's thinking, "Hey, is there a story here? Maybe, maybe not."

Then the years evaporate like steam shooting out of a kettle
and the stories have not been found or never existed
as they are now in fact in a vacuum somewhere around here
where there was an explosion in space a couple of decades ago
or something similar happened to me that was about
half an entire century old or more than half.

In 1942 the time changed all the time
but it wasn't until we got there that we realized
the difference between the ages and what it meant
in terms of how much it actually changed.
Replacing a guard in a guard tower with a lover
does not make a trusted friend.
To trust in such a time is a great way to protect the relationship
between your friend or your family members
who may have lost their loved ones in the process of becoming
a member of a group of people who have never
met a stranger or seen one before.

There was waiting and later the waiting would still be there
but with little at stake: say a state of convenience
caused by the presence of raw walnuts,
organic peanut butter that won't break the bank
even as the banks break under their own weight.

All the barracks looked the same except for the inside
where slightly different utensils were stored
in slightly different ways, chopsticks placed
upside down in a cup, or laid flat in a drawer
next to the forks and knives.
Even a shirt mislaid on the bed can signal home,
release a chemical in the brain that floods the body,
making it remember the couch in front of the TV
of their childhood home, before the idea
of rising home prices and mortgage interest rates

and inflation entered the vocabulary,
back when myth took your breath away
and it was all the opposite of financial literacy
and useful education versus a terrible waste of time,
such as when one reads about epistemology.
You lost me at theory of knowledge
and the science of the universe in general
but you still got the basics of it all together.

David Mura

●●●●●●●

Letters from Poston Relocation Camp (1942–45)

Dear Michiko,

Do songs sound different in prison?
I think there are more spaces between the words.
I think, when the song ends, the silence
does not stop singing. I think
there is nothing but song.

Matsuo's back, his bruises almost healed,
a tooth missing. His *biwa*
comes out again with the stars, a nightly
matter. He sends his regards.

Do you get fed these putrid gray beans?
I hope you haven't swallowed too
many of them. They put my stomach
in a permanent revolt, shouting no emperor
would ever feed his people so harshly.
I agree. Let's you and I grow
skinny together. Let's keep the peace.

Any second the lights will go off.

I look around me and see many
honest men who hide their beauty
as best they can.

I think that's what the whites hate,
our beauty, the way we carry the land
and the life of plants inside us,
seedlings and fruit, the flowers
and the flush tree, fields freed of weeds.

Why can't they see the door's inside them?
If someone found an answer to that,
they'd find an answer to why
those who are hungry and cold
go off to battle to become hungrier
and colder, farther from home.

Nine o'clock. The lights all out.

~

Dear Michiko,

Did you hear it last night?
So many cries
clinging to the wind?

Not just the grinding
of tanks, rifles and mortars,
or the sound of eyelids
closing forever, but something
hungrier, colder.

I'm frightened. So many dying.
What do our complaints
about blankets or late letters
matter? Or even our dreams?

But this was more than a dream.

It came across seas
and the mountains,
it smelled of ash, a gasless flame,
and I woke this morning
still tired, irritable, unable to rise.

Later, bending to
the tomatoes, in line to mess,
trudging through the desert dust,
the sun plowing its furrows
on my neck, I thought

I heard them again. The cries.

I wanted to answer: my lips
were cracked, dry.

Michiko,
am I going crazy?
Did you hear them?

~

...Sometimes, Michiko,
I think of my greenhouse,
how I used to stand at night in its fleshy,
steaming dark and say, "These are the most
beautiful orchids and roses in the world."
And their fragrance seeped inside me,
stayed even when I sold them.

What is it like now in Tokyo?
They say it has
sunk like a great ship.

Forgive me. Blessed
with a chance to talk to my wife,

more beautiful than any greenhouse rose,
all I can do is moan.
And yet, if I didn't tell you,
I would be angry at you for not listening,
blaming you for what I haven't spoken.

And it's too late for that...

When you write back, please
tell me what country I'm in.

I feel so poor now.
These words are all I own.

Garrett Hongo

• • • • • • • • • • •

Kubota to Miguel Hernández in Heaven, Leupp, Arizona, 1942

The sun travels slowly from over the top of this adobe stockade
And, when I finally wake and pull my face to the bars
At my window, I see a gray light filling the shadows
Between the mess and the guard quarters
And among river stones on the sides of the central well.
Horses snort and whinny far off from the corral I cannot see,
And a line of burrows shuffles by, led by a single Navajo
Dressed khaki-colored clothes from the trading post.
I've been here two months now, can name the hills
Surrounding this plateau of piñion pines—words I learned
From the guards and other prisoners, Japanese like me
Swept up in the days after the attack on Pearl Harbor.
The guards won't say what our crime is, rarely address us,
But I overhear them sometimes, saying the names of mountains,
Nearby towns, complaining about food and us "Japs."
They won't say if we'll be let go. The interrogators come
Every few days and ask about our hobbies back home—
Studying poetry, working the shortwave radio at night,
And me, how I go night fishing for *kumu* on Kahuku Point.
What landed me here was I used to go torching,
Wrapping the kerosene-soaked rags on bamboo poles,
Sticking them into the sand inside the lagoon,
And then go light them with a flick from my Zippo.
The fish come in from outside the reef,
Schooling to the light, and me I catch enough
To feed my neighbors—Portagee, Hawai'ian, Chinee, and all—

Eating good for days after, like New Year's in early December.
For this they say I'm signaling submarines offshore,
Telling the Japanese navy the northernmost landfall on the island.
That's a lie. They ask when—I tell them. They ask where—I tell them.
How many fish —I tell them same every time. No change my answer.
But how can you transform your sorrow into poems, Miguel?
To think of your wife and infant son with only onions to eat,
While you sing your lullabies from your cell in Alicante?
Is it cold for you, Miguel? With only the dark to wrap yourself in?
Is it warm, even hot here on Navajo land in northern Arizona,
Where your poems descend to me in the moon's sweet, silver light
As it rises over the Mogollon Plateau these summer evenings.
They say that your sentence was death for writing poetry,
That you celebrated the Republic and the commoners.
I celebrated only my family and the richness of the sea.
My sentence, therefore, is only eternity to wait, not knowing,
Imagining *everything,* imagining nothing—
My wife taking in boarders, doing their laundry and sewing,
My children growing more trivial by the day
Without word where I have been taken,
Whether I will be returned or simply have vanished
Into the unwritten history of our country.
Your suffering tells me to be patient, Miguel,
To think of your song of sweet onions lulling your baby,
Even in his hunger, to a peaceful sleep,
While the wars of our time, and their ignorant ministrations,
Go on shedding their black, tyrannical light into the future.

Kubota to Nâzım Hikmet in Peredelkino, Moscow, from Leupp, Arizona

I learned a sheepherder's stew last week, Nâzim.
Navajos taught me to make it from scraps
Of lamb from the mess, onions from the army's bags,
And pine nuts I picked from the pinon trees on the walks
They allow me from time to time.

Hawks circling above,
A stray's carcass on the ground crawling with maggots,
A patch of mesquite, and blue clouds like Portuguese men-of-war
Stringing tentacles of rain across the far distance of the red-rock
plateau around me.

I think of home too much, allow sorrow to swell in my throat
Whenever I hear the chatter of finches or the whirr of chukar flushed
from the sages.
I recall my days hiding in stands of strawberry guava,
Hunting for plover in the grassy patches along the low ridges of the
Ko'olaus above the cane fields.

My 12-gauge made me feel I owned property like I was *haole,*
My shots with it brought down dinners of wild game for Sunday table.
Walking back home, down through the grass fields for cattle,
Jumping the irrigation ditches like sluices like a *luna wai,*
I felt like I was boss of things, a manager, and could dream any future,
Quiet cane fires in my heart, fresh mountain rains washing clean
all the confusions of the day.

But when they slop me like I was pig and shove me
Into this dusty cell with no floor but the desert,
I can think of nothing but the pain of this dull light
Leaking in through the bars of my cell window,

And I hear the grind of a Jeep stalled in mud,
Or the shallow peeps of beggar birds asking for crumbs
From the guards and the innocent, passing Navajos
Going in and out of the post with their daily ease.
Murmuring their soft language of chuffs and whispers.

How can a man move from splendor to prison so swiftly
And learn to nurse his own soul in this abandonment?
You chronicle by the day, Nâzim, all the things you have loved—
The lacing touch of your wife's fingertips across your lips,
The fall of her veil across her face, your blue Polish eyes,
The tea you drink in little cups with her in her afternoons,
The quiet bells and padding of footsteps on a merchant street.

You sweeten the tenderness of your own soul in isolation, Nâzim,
In the face of accusations, in answer to questions from the unforgiving.
To a slap, you return a smile; to a fist, you give a kiss; to torturers,
You write poems planning the planting of an olive tree when you are
    seventy!

My way adds a little pain each day, though my captors are not rough.
They give me potatoes, toss me their leftover fruits, light my cigarette.
But I quail like a bird when I think too much, fluttering in my soul
The escaping wings that are the withering of hope and who I used to
    be—
Proud father and storekeeper, husband to Tsuruko,
And grandkeeper of loans and accounts for Lā'ie village.

*

I can give no tenderness to myself within these walls,
Only scratch my name and quote a saying from a poem
On the day the DOJ first brought me here to Leupp.

When you saw the blue sky that one day in Istanbul, Nâzim,
How could you lie down on the ground and look up to it?
In respectful devotion to its full immensity?

Teach me this—
To think only of the white wall I lean on next to me,
As you did, to forget Anatolia, your home, and Hawai'i, mine,
To grieve only for an instant for the waves of the sea we have lost,
For the freedom and the preciousness of our lonely wives.
Teach me the soil, Nâzim, the sun and the time, as babies,
Born in strife, that they first took us into it.

Jodi Hottel

•••••••

A Few Seeds

What instinct told me
my heart would need
those tiny packets of seeds
smuggled in my pockets—
cucumber, zinnia,
pea and chrysanthemum—
even more than I'd need a coat
to shield me from the bitter winds
of a desert winter?

A few seeds sown in improbable soil
beside barbed wire,
vigilantly watered using
tin cans from the mess hall garbage,
till tender shoots peeked
above ground
reaching
for the meager
warmth
of April.

Now, rambunctious morning glory vines
tangle with cucumber,
climb tarpaper walls
to disguise my bleak barrack.
Snowy mums and golden zinnias waken
and nod their noble heads to me.

I stroll in the shadow
of a guard tower
as the desert heat softens to dusk.
In block after block
green patches of wonder
are sprouting,
cultivated by those,
like me,
who thrust into coat pockets
tiny packets of hope.

Ryan Hitoshi Nakano

●●●●●●●●●●●●●●●

Stolen

after Florence Nakano Tsunoda—An Oral History

They took my car. And now
they wonder why I hunt

laughing the man cuts open a rattlesnake
this isn't hunting he says

hunting is what they did after sinking
their teeth into our skin

his daughter peels back a floorboard
to reveal a snake pit under the barracks

we're making medicine by studying its venom
we think the blood might thicken

we think if we gather enough of them and run
experiments we might self-determine

a field mouse seeking shelter from the desert
falls into the opening made by the woman

its cheeks full of grass seed soften
under a slow release of hemotoxin

sister scribbles a single word
into her notebook: why

I'm gardening says the other
a stream of snakes take turns leaving

slow releasing seeds
back into the earth's surface

two boys come in from outside
their eyes   swirling gas giants

Papa   the dust never settled
did you try blinking

we can't
we've lost our eyelids

Kiik Araki-Kawaguchi

evening song

Yoshikane Araki did all he could to temper his desire for the tower guard, but the evening song of the guard would not be interrupted by earplugs of clay or beeswax, by tissue or cotton packing, and continued to pierce Kane's dreams, once inside surging like the ghost-pollen of creosote poppies, and in the morning he awoke mouthing those bewildering words, tongue slack with ghost-breath, a rawness, soreness, the vague belief the sentry's mouth had been all night pinned over his own.

an ocean

Yoshikane Araki was conceived in 1943 near the southeast barracks atop a frayed blanket spread over scorpion molt and scalding desert stones, and as Youko Araki carried him through those torrid months, she spoke to him through her belly of her family's home beside the coastline, the aroma of the sea strong as an arrangement of sour flowers held to her face, the monstrous blacklip abalone clinging within rocky crevasses, the feral dogs who burrowed in saltmud and tore through sand crabs, all she could remember, every gull song and whale song, every sea succulent and blossom, and on the day of Kane's birth, when Youko opened her legs to deliver, an entire ocean rushed forth and submerged the Gila Relocation, the hospital, the mess hall, the chapel, the barracks overrun by whelk and toxic jelly and sardine, so that it took her three days' search by rowboat to recover the infant Kane, found swaddled in kelp and froth and fish spittle, sucking the coil of a limpet as though it was his mother's nipple.

doorway of blossoms

Margaret Morri was a rugrat when she carried to Gila River a single clingstone, pried from a yellow Tulare peach, stone she held like an amulet in her sleep, stone to be activated in the center of her fist, in her dreams Margaret watched the stone grow flesh, flesh that orbited her skull, flesh that crawled through the skull's electricity and caught fire, bubbled over with sugar, hissed sweetness from its nearby flowers, a whiskered peel becoming flush in the desert sun, Margaret waking one morning to discover the stone lodged in the barrack floorboards beside her, fractured hull giving way to radicle and plumule, shoot splitting from axil, sapling spreading into new fluttering leaves, and upon a subsequent morning, a yellow Tulare peach pumping like a heart in Margaret's palm, hot to the touch, ambrosial, and over the next three years in camp, the Morri family barracks gradually inhabited by the marriage of stone and dream, Margaret's parents, Masahiro and Mariko Morri, having to step over or kick away clumps of flocculent roots, having to stoop to the nearly snapping branches descending from the barrack's roof beams, and though relatives warned of tiger beetles and red harvester ants, though Margaret's brothers complained of the yellow peach tree's debris littering their hair, the tree sap staining their shirts, the Morris never allowed so much as a penknife to be raised in the direction of the spreading branches and every night continued to be drawn into campaigns of flicking earwigs out of the doorway of blossoms.

shō yamagushiku

•••••••••••••

The Frozen Native

as vast is the night sky so is his forgetting
a man so lost he is not permitted sleep
each night comes and he is thrown
from the barracks into this ocean of sand
there are no clouds in the sky and still the stars don't shine
sounds of english and japanese
are broken glass dust shards clogging his lungs
classmates mocking laughs that cursed
him with a broken tongue broken island
broken boy. thrown back and forth in bewilderment
last night they hung him, shimanchu boy, island still
    wet on his tongue,
on a pole in the mess hall all the naichi boys

together they tossed leftovers and excrement
until he was coated in shame
drowning in their fears he understands
his loneliness carves it into his wrists as non-existence.
the desert is silent and so are his ancestors
future ones came and rescued the others
but he waits in purgatory screaming and screaming
watta shima ya maa yaga?
watta uyaa maa yaga?
–the last speaker of his language left alive

it is a python far from home
escaped from a ship that travelled from guangdong
to okinawa, freeing itself in the ports of california

sent eastward into the desert horizon
the snake finds the boy's body
and begins to wrap himself around
what will soon become a corpse constricting
his pain devouring his sadness

75 years later i return to the desert
to this memorial for incarceration
and find their bodies–the boy and the snake
embracing in wind swept dunes flesh
still rotting and as if waiting for me
the snake skin slips free
from bone and like some old ancestral psalm
i fashion it taut over my water canister and the
boy's hair becomes strings that stretch from neck
to tip / a sanshin conjured from teachings that time
forgot a memory lodged somewhere else

i begin to pluck the strings

and with the sad song rain begins
to pour down that once in a decade torrent
and this arid desert might as well
be tomigusuku or kin-town or chatan for the monsoon
has obscured all proof of place and as
a cactus bloom a song springs forth
and from the corners of manzanar
and rohwer and jerome and poston a weight is lifted
on every shimanchu soul silenced

[a vastness]

a vastness

disappears

abandons me

to a cloudless night

all the stars

turn sleep's path

against me

in the distance, nikkei boys

loosen laughter

an island blowing

hot and brassy

from my

tongue

Terry Watada

●●●●●●●●●●

Moon Above the Ruins

for hisashi goromaru
Hiroshima-ken
1910–1987

Tashme, B.C.
1942–1945

There is only the moon
above
    the ruins
  of Tashme.

Takeo came out
of his internment cabin
playing his *shakuhachi*
a mournful tune

    blowing dry through the bamboo
    tunnel of that instrument,

minor notes bent to the wind
rose to the parched, mad moon
during that early august

one by one
the other prisoners
emerged
into the dry light

looking for the sun
that was never
to rise again

we sought
the warmth of each other

we knew that time
was over.

one by one
    we left the camp
and ventured in-
to the cool mountain
breezes

that came down and blew
through our shrinking selves.

arid cracked voices drew
together and rode
bareback
            on the hollow notes
of that old flute
until the rock mountain
faces
            sang back to us
an ancient pentatonic
song

there is only the moon,
since the august sun
exploded over hiroshima,

burning paper cranes
and freezing shadows
    during the cusp of
    sunrise
    and moonset.

Cathlin Goulding

Toy Library

During the war, they built a toy library for the children in the camps. The library was divided into sections: A toy lending room and two rooms for play.

The camps had created an unnatural home situation, the administrators reported. A lending library of toys would foster fairness, sportsmanship, and timely return of loans.

The children in the camps did not care for the war games that appealed to children outside. They liked jacks. Tiddlywinks. Dominoes.

When the toy library opened, the children waited patiently. They filled out a card with their name, date, and the condition of the object. They selected blinking ivory dolls.

Years after the camps closed, the buildings dismantled, archeologists discovered glass marbles. The marbles surfaced in remote areas, away from prisoners' living quarters.

The location of the marbles, the archaeologists determined, indicated the places for children's play. Places far from the purview of adults.

As a child, my mother said she was the king of the schoolyard. The master of marbles. In the weeks after her funeral, I found a Folgers coffee can in the back of a drawer.

My mother's marbles: yellow, blue, and rainbow swirls. I rolled them in my palm and pressed the cool glass to my cheek.

In his 1988 study, *Children and Play and the Holocaust: Games Among the Shadows,* George Eisen explains play in the camps confirms "one of the deepest instincts in the human mind."

Even when play is limited, Eisen wrote, children would establish a "defensive perimeter." In the camps, children would insist on their agency.

In the toy library, the logic of the camp was undone. The totalizing decimation, the academic theorizing, was now defunct. I considered the diffusion of agency, the poststructural turn.

In the toy library, I did less. I did nothing. Nothing appealed to me. My aims became subtler. My ambitions were stilted. My analysis turned sour, absurd.

In the toy library, my mother was not to be disturbed. She picked out a cowboy hat, spurs for her two-toned boots, and a plastic horse with a curry comb.

In the toy library, I upended the procedure. I argued with well-meaning civil servants. I slashed cards in the catalog. I refused stated policies. I turned in items late.

In the toy library, my mother settled on a set of pistols. She twirled them. She caressed the ivory handles. She checked the safety.

In the toy library, my mother assessed the situation. She saw who obeyed. Who dissented. She saw me. And she aimed.

Sharon Hashimoto

• • • • • • • • • • • • • • •

Smithsonian Natural Museum of American History, *A More Perfect Union: Japanese Americans and the US Constitution*

My walk is slow among the black-and-white
photographs, so many shots of the same landscape
with different names: Manzanar, Minidoka, Gila River.
The same pictures of the evacuation order nailed
to buildings and telephone poles. Too young
to have been sent there myself, I pass another portrait
then stop, and turn back. This one of men
in fedoras and overalls, sweatered mothers
in line with kids. Suddenly, *you're* there—
the teen-ager ladling chili into a bowl.
Have you been sent back to stand over
the steaming pot? A placard on the wall
behind you says "dinner is served cafeteria style
at the Heart Mountain Relocation Center."
This is you, who now tells me you don't
remember much except sagebrush and coal
for the pot-bellied stove. Hair edges
into your eyes and you tilt your head down.
Nothing matters but the stripes on cuff
and collar of the baseball jacket you wear.
Careful not to spill when you give back the bowl,
do you look at the face of the hand that takes it?

George Uba

●●●●●●●●

Old Photo, 1942

My father, fresh out of dental school,
decked out in short sleeves
and baggy slacks, his hair
cropped too short near the ears,
stands close to my mother,
his arm secretly about her waist.
My mother in white blouse and skirt,
in white bobby socks, in loafers
pressed together in a regimental line,
looks like a pretty schoolgirl
politely waiting for a bus.
They have recently become engaged,
hence the liberty my father takes.

Back of them is a double row
of barracks silently fronting
a perfectly level, unpaved space.
I know what is behind each door:
an iron stove of the kind
they no longer make,
a card table and folding chairs,
an improvised bookshelf,
and an army-issue bed
topped by the same stuff
the curtains are made of.

There is no military base.
There is recycled wood

stapled at angles to form rooms;
in the rooms are lives named
Tanaka, Funakoshi, Uba,
and pictures of loved ones
not yet eligible for war.
From the window there is a glimpse
of a gun emplacement, of a gun
secretly raking my parents
from the deck of a watchtower,
while, off in the distance,
over my mother's shoulder,
rises a solitary peak, Heart Mountain,
that my father could easily
cup in one hand.

All of this covers less
than half the photograph.
The rest is sky, Wyoming sky,
that, because of a trick of light,
appears the exact color of rust.

Dawn in the Internment Camp at Heart Mountain

Wyoming, 1943

Someone clever has carved a deer
out of a scrap of wood
and set it on a table or shelf
inside a shabby room among a file
of barracks, along a street of sleep.
In its miniature dawn, its hues
are gradually revealed,
its legs regain their poise,
its eyes open. Someone clever
has set a mountain in the backyard
beyond the barracks and morning's incipient din,
to loom above the density of human emotions,
to relieve the clutter of stars overhead.
And—just now it beckons to the deer.

Kevin Irie

•••••••

Tashme

Lay the wood
in the fireplace now.
Ignite those feelings
smouldering still from the memory of Tashme,
that very first winter.

Memory holds to the site of those homes,
uniform rows of wooden shacks,
government timber
shipped inland
abruptly
as you,
            those upright
generations
cut.

Cabin walls beaded
with condensation, blankets
damp as if fevered,
the few books moist as those logs out back,
the wood that was green,
too wet,
not cured,
that gave little warmth
when placed in the stove
but just enough light to offer a glimpse
of how hard the winter ahead would be.

Remember how children wept from the cold,
while grown-ups whispered, *It can't be helped,*
their words: kindling
lit in a blizzard,
wood's weak voice
in the family stove

where the wet fuel popped and sizzled flat.

Remember the evenings bolted inside,
where the household banter
said you were safe,
how even the clang of an empty kettle
could jar a memory of a kitchen on Powell Street,
how one plate carried
the weight of home,
how hands washed rice
like surf rolling gravel
while mother and father
presided at meals
and neighbours on the other side of the wall
bickered about the cold, the law.
Their voice was everything
your parents would not speak.

But you speak it now,
to your children, theirs,
though Tashme is almost a word snuffed out,
a site in the Cascades
cleared off maps
along with Bayfarm, Popoff, Sandon,
memory solid as the ice
that clamped your shoes to the floor by morning,
sharper than the memory
of home on the coast.

A memory

cured and dry as timber,
a funeral pyre.

Your mother and father both gone now.

And Tashme

never warm enough in winter,

still can sear

and burn.*

* Tashme was the name of an interment camp for Japanese-Canadians during World War II. Located fourteen miles from Hope, British Columbia, it was surrounded by the Cascade Mountain Range.

The Camps: Burning The Dead

Because there was no undertaker,
no place
allotted to the dead
as yet,

inmates had to cremate
each body
as quickly as possible,
recruiting
boys
to watch the pyre
which often took all night to burn.

It was their job
to guard the corpse,
stoke the flames
when the fires bled low,

each one serving
an hour's endurance
then relieved, and coming back

with ashes
sewn so deep in their clothes
that finally those garments
were burned as well.

Now, years later,
it is another memory
that men retain
but seldom tell,

tailored
in their suits

at another funeral,

their past

still sewn deep in their skin.

Amy Uyematsu

●●●●●●●●●●●

36 Views of Manzanar

among those taken away, my father's family
the Francis M. Uyematsus of Montebello

1

How can a name be
so lovely but cruel:
Manzanar, the Spanish word
for apple orchard.

2

Manzanar, the first to open—
March of '42, Roosevelt
even uses the term
concentration camp, soon
replacing it with
the "more acceptable"
WRA relocation centers.

3

Camp equation:

540 acres + 8 guard towers + 36 blocks
= 10,046 prisoners

4

Summer days, over 110, winters below freezing
and that unending wind
drowning prisoners in dust and sand.

5

How often life depends
on political connections—
even in camp—My father
knows Paul Bannai,
a nisei buddy
with an early camp job.

Dad wrangles a deal
where the Uyematsus
originally assigned
to Heart Mountain
go to Manzanar instead.

Grandpa must donate
cherry trees in exchange
for moving to a camp
in California, not Wyoming,
less than 5 hours' drive
from Grandpa's nurseries.

6

Aunt Mare, now 92, the only
surviving Uyematsu internee

recalls being 15 and driven
to Manzanar in a government car.

There were 36 blocks and

first, the family lives in block 36

then re-assigned to 6-10-2
block 6 building 10 apartment 2

close to the laundry room
and the women's latrine.

7

Tar paper–covered barracks
with holes and slits
in the walls and doors—

Aunt Mare remembers
dirt piling up in the windows
and having to go outside
to shake sand out
from the bedding.

8

The next time you reach for
a Dr. Seuss book,
remember that Theodor Seuss Geisel
depicted Japanese as monster hordes

one cartoon shows "Jap Alley"
with Uncle Sam being attacked
by a mob of slant-eyed cats
carrying the imperial flag.

9

My own Uncle Sam,
only 9 years old in Manzanar,
remembers the tiny

rooms for families
and toilets squeezed together
with no stalls or partitions—

is Grandma one of the women
who make late-night trips
to the latrine for privacy
or who travel in pairs
holding up coats
as makeshift doors.

10

Many internees work
in camp, including Dad
who, early on, gets to pick
from a list just because
he's Paul Bannai's pal.

Dad's task: go through
stacks of books dropped off
by Army trucks as camp
gets ready to open school
and a library.

He's paid 12 bucks per month
and with three others
organizes the books—
describing it as
an "easy job."

11

Mess hall meals
are just that—a mess—

long lines

long tables
lousy food

parental authority
gone as kids run wild
teens escape boredom.

12

Only natural that the issei,
who excel as farmers,
nurserymen, flower growers,
will soon figure out

how to grow produce
design gardens and ponds
genius at coaxing green
from this dry desert soil

they even have contests
for the most beautiful
barracks garden—
the first winner, Block 34.

13

The Tomita boys crawl
under the barbed wire fencing
to go fishing at George Creek
with poles made from willow
and paper clip hooks
to catch rainbow trout.

So do others, as many as 400,
slipping out of camp for a day
or as long as two weeks—

Part of the challenge
to escape the armed guards
posted at watchtowers—
fresh trout and
temporary freedom
the delicious rewards.

14

Dad doesn't talk much about Manzanar
obtains a permit as soon as he can
to work farms in Utah and Idaho
harvesting sugar beets and potatoes

but he tells me about Aunt Alice
who's never able to enjoy her teens
she comes down with TB and after
release from camp, never recovers.

15

Within six months of opening, protests
and what authorities claim as a "riot,"
guards shooting into a crowd of 500.

James Ito from Los Angeles, only 17,
the first camp casualty—shot
through the abdomen and heart—his

mother dressed in the vest
James wears when he's killed,
a vest with a hole in the back.

16

Toyo Miyatake, already a well-known
photographer before the war,

manages to smuggle a camera lens
and film plate holder into Manzanar.

At first taking pictures in secret, he
believes it's his duty to record camp life—
eventually Toyo is allowed
to be "official" camp photographer.

In one well-known shot, three boys
look out through the barbed wire,
in another, he poses his son holding
a pair of clippers against the fence.

17

There is even a monthly
newspaper in English—
everything from birth
and death announcements
to camp baseball team scores
and ads for Sears Roebuck—
dark humor in its title,
the "Manzanar Free Press."

18

Remember who profit most
from putting Japanese behind barbed wire:
the Hearst corporation,
white farmers who want the acres
our issei have transformed
into fertile farmland,
neighbors who loot households
vacated during the camp years,
businessmen like Manchester Boddy
who buys Grandpa's total inventory,
over 300,000 camellias,

far below what they're worth—
or as Dad puts it, Boddy plunders
Grandpa's plants "for a song."

19

Not even a full year
when internees
must answer
a loyalty questionnaire—

A "yes" on #27 means
you're willing
to fight in
US armed forces

A "yes" on #28 means
you swear unqualified
allegiance to the country
that's locked you up

One Manzanar internee's
response: "What
do they know
about loyalty?"

20

July 27, 1942 front page
from the Manzanar Free Press:
"Mrs. Karl Yoneda, 4-2-2,
who, singlehanded, produced
four nets per day"
breaking a record
at the camouflage factory.

21

In high school Aunt Mare joins
a girls' club—the Wee Funsters
that parties with handsome guys
who belong to the Manza-Knights,

she remembers Ralph Lazo—
doesn't find out till camp is over
Ralph isn't Japanese but chooses
to join his nisei high school friends.

22

By September of '42
only 26 of the 57
white teachers hired
to work at Manzanar
show up—

the qualified evacuees
used as aides
to fill in the gap
earn $16 a month,
teachers, $135.

23

Tatsuo Kunitomi, aged 12, asks
his sister— "What's the use
of studying American history
when we're behind barbed wire?"

24

Only 14, Hank Umemoto looks out
his barrack window—a majestic Mt. Whitney

against an indigo sky—vowing
one day to climb to the top.

He never forgets his promise—
reaching the mountain summit,
over 14,000 feet high,
at the unlikely age of 71.

25

Baseball, basketball, and more
for both kids and adults
Team names like the Yahoodies,
Manza-Bombers, Aloha Ramblers

Monikers like "Puk" and "Boots"
and "Pardon My Looks"

Sports already common in J-A life
even more essential in prison camp.

26

At Mom's retirement home
I interview Frank Kikuchi—
a nisei deejay at Manzanar.

Smiling, Frank recounts how
he and buddy Archie Miyatake
played those '40s big band hits—

Jimmy Dorsey, Glenn Miller—
so kids can jitterbug
and slow dance.

Refreshments include
Kool-Aid punch

and egg salad sandwiches.

27

August is the month of obon—
a Buddhist festival to honor
the ancestral spirits—

Even at Manzanar in 1942
and by the next year
thousands turning out

To watch 1600 dancers
clad in colorful kimonos
join the bon odori circle.

28

Grandpa trucks in cherry trees
from his Montebello nursery

for a garden constructed
outside the Children's Village.

Manzanar's orphanage includes
kids from white foster families,

infants as young as 6 months,
children from Alaska to San Diego

Army Col. Bendetsen says, "if they
have one drop of Japanese blood."

For many of the 101 wards
camp is the first family they know.

At war's end many have

no guardian to claim them

and Grandpa never finds out
where his cherry trees end up.

29

Just six miles north,
the town closest
to Manzanar
is named Independence.

30

24 years later
the first annual
Manzanar pilgrimage—

nisei survivors
sansei activists
paying homage—

a tradition
carried on
since 1969.

31

An interfaith obelisk
is built in the cemetery
to honor the deceased—
Buddhists and Christians together,
each family donating
ten to fifteen cents each
to purchase concrete—

"Ireito" inscribed

in black kanji characters,
“soul consoling tower”
their literal translation—
the white stone monument
still stands after
seventy-seven years.

32

In 1992 Manzanar is named
a national historic site—
exactly 50 years after FDR
signs the executive order
rounding up 120,000
innocent Japanese Americans.

Visitors can now walk through
reconstructed barracks,
younger generations locating
our grandparents’ names
from the thousands listed
in alphabetical order.

33

Questions I wish
I could ask
my issei grandparents,
Francis and Kuniko
who don’t speak English,
who don’t live long enough
to hear the President’s apology:

Grandpa, did you find
comfort tending to your
cherry trees, watering
your wisteria—

and Grandma, did you keep
writing tanka, your feelings
about camp?

34

Scores of books
from history to memoir:
"Farewell to Manzanar"
in the high school
curriculum where I teach—

But still, too many voices
unheard, too many stories
that will never be told.

35

The collective chant
at Manzanar pilgrimages:
"Don't Repeat History."

After 9/11, pilgrimages
include Muslims
who've become targets.

Recent calls grow even louder
as migrant families are separated,
children imprisoned in border jails.

36

When my Uncle Sam turns 70,
we talk about driving
to Manzanar together
to visit the camp after
so many decades—

he dies before
we ever get the chance.

Mia Ayumi Malhotra

Portrait of Isako in Wartime

Ohio, and I imagine her
    walking the train line,
tracks narrowed in the distance.
    Through her soles,
the platform's slats. She feels
    their unevenness
in the flats of her feet. Noon-
    day heat and the wool
of her jacket's itchy.
    She's got a bob, it's 1943
and the war's on. No one
    in the station looks
like her, but everyone's
    looking at her.
No explanation but the one
    in government-issued print.
National Student Relocation
    Council. *Early Release.*
The sentry in his watch-
    tower, barbed-wire fence
and Stars and Stripes flapping
    in the wind. From across
the tracks, a man (here,
    imagination does the work
history's lost) approaches, finger
    bared, a blunt accusation.
Aren't you a *Jap?* The long
    explanation—why she's out,

whose side she's on.
    The nations we pledge
at odds, leaving us to make
    up the difference.
This story's old, the woman
    —dead, papers boxed
in a back closet. I've seen them.
    Early Release.
The government-issued ID number.

    In camp, it's said, they cut
gardens into Arkansas desert,
    fixed rocks into the flat face
of the earth and irrigated
    bean rows to feed their families.
Healthy vines appeared
    where none should have
grown; tiny buds coaxed
    from the earth, tendrils
that spooled runners
    through dust.
When the order came
    to pack up and return
home, the authorities found
    every curtain drawn
shut. Every barrack
    floor swept clean.

Christine Kitano

●●●●●●●●●●●●

1945: My Father Leaves Topaz Internment Camp, Utah

At war's end, my father, nineteen,
rode the train from Salt Lake to Milwaukee
to take a job killing cows—for that one year
he stopped eating meat.

If you strike, he said, the hollow
between the animal's eyes, and if the ax is right,
the pain is quick. The cow's heavy collapse
the worst sound he'd remember.

When the families were herded
into trains with unknown destinations,
my grandmother dressed her children
in their best clothes, in case
they were being taken away to be shot.
She might have shrugged when she saw
the neighbors, dressed in rags
for the same uncertainty.

David Mura

•••••••

Internment Camp Psychology

circa 1945

Just after his release Mas took a psychological test.

Three questions he never forgot: Do you think

people are out to get you? Do you feel you are

being followed? When you see a crowd of strangers

walking toward you, do you try to avoid them?

To all three he answered yes.

And knew he sounded insane.

Heather Nagami

● ● ● ● ● ● ● ● ● ● ● ●

After Poston, East Los Angeles, 1946

as told by Auntie Chiyo

I would glance around the classroom
and the other kids would be drawing
so many different places, their minds
a rainbow of crayon confetti, crafting
so many different objects.

But every day
I would draw
the same

mountains, sky, blank
desert. I didn't
understand, but
that was all
I could
think

mountains

sky

blank

desert

every

day.

III
Each Leaf / Remembers

● ● ● ● ● ● ● ● ●

each leaf
remembers the feeling of branches

—**Micah Tasaka**,
"Tree (why my father didn't teach me Japanese)"

Brittany Arita

●●●●●●●●●●

?

if you were still here
would i have the courage
to even ask

or would i remain
a *question*
mark-ed by history

W. Todd Kaneko

●●●●●●●●●●●●

ghost story

1.
A child walks through
a closed door.

2.
Not a child but everyone
in my family—
all walking all the time without seeing
where we've come from.

3.
Everyone in my family is dead,
except for those who are still
alive amen amen
to bring the dead back to us.

4.
My grandmother is no longer alive,
and she tells me stories at night
about Minidoka, about Idaho—
amen amen

5.
My grandfather is no longer alive,
and he tells me stories about my grandmother.
amen amen They say this is how the lioness
was turned into a witch. They say

there is no such thing as magic—
amen amen

6.
My father is no longer alive,
and he tells me stories about life
in a concentration camp.

They say this is how life is
breathed into a body,   amen amen
how it feels to be out of breath.

7.
One day the child will grow up and tell me
a story about Idaho, how my family learned
to pray, how in the end
no one remembers how to pray.

8.
One day the door will open
and so many stories spill forth.
They say this is where our hearts are buried.
They say this is how the crows learned our names.
They say Minidoka over and over again
so that my family can finally sleep.

9.
There is no child,
there is no door—
one day my son will ask me
where we come from   amen amen
and no one will be there
to tell us the answer.

Starr Sumie Miyata

•••••••••••••••

Self Portrait; Family Portrait

the parting of two black doves
                                                  over

a red sun

                              just,

                                        the parting

Emily Mitamura

●●●●●●●●●●●●

Self-Portrait as Contained Swarm

My body metabolizes stress as dreams about bed bugs.
Indoor space is a biome scientists are still learning how to know.
I flip bedsheets inside out
and exclude you from the poem.

After camp, my grandmother hoarded every thing.
This new branch of urban ecology reproduces in built structures.
A professor advised me once to fall in love.
A cell changes over time.

Each time I'm touched
like peeping through my skin is clear domicile.
I know homemaking is a weapon.
Silverfish aren't fish. Too   alive at the gut.

My friend asks me what I think of minimalism.
My grandmother picked horse lice out of my uncle Yoshio's hair
    a holding.
I've been tempted by the idea of empty space.
I lock myself up at night since then.

Human houses are only a subset of the indoor biome, not including
    animal stalls.
The indoor biome is suited for citizen science.
My grandmother used to live here.
We inhabit each other, a definition of affect I'm trying on for myself.

I read the flora and fauna in my home as uncannily resilient.

My ancestors' bodies were presciently small.
Nests accommodate the needs of infestation.
I simply could not live in this house alone.

Even minimally, after disrepair, my body is built of course.
A cell changes over time.
Arthropods have been domesticated, we didn't know, flattening
themselves to the home.
I'm learning how to name a space I wish was empty.

My now partner does not laugh at me peeling my skin at a swarm
in our house.
There is a minimalism to keeping my self inside.
A hoard reproduces itself along a family line, diverging
form and association.
A cell changes over time.

I want to exclude you from the poem.
The house is crawling.
Bedsheets might be a dried expanse.
Empty space, the unseen   within and beneath the home, must be
cared for—stands in relation, if abhorred.

I hoard myself a swarm.
The ecosystem of my house requires the materiality of my living.
I am as fruitful as I am indebted.
My grandma used to live here.

I still can't stand my own un-empty sound.
A single organism working isn't a house alive.
Evolution happens to me.
As if   that is love.

My grandma is a swarm.
I love a swarm.
I could be a biome.
Indeed, I am.

Laura K. Fukumoto

Lucky

Crisp leaves crunching 'neath my feet,
The tang of pine trees in the air,
A winding trail and a rustic seat
And winter stirring in its lair.

The mossy trees on the barren heights,
The honking geese on their homeward flight,
A cold wind riffling thru my hair,
All these whisper – "Autumn's here!"
—"Walking Through Autumn Woods" was written orally and remembered (until she finally wrote it down at age 100) by Kiyo Kay Fukumoto, while incarcerated in Slocan Valley, B.C.

1.
I don't know much
but I know my name

means "wellspring of luck"
which is what Brother Iwaasa, small rock of a man, said to me while
my peers watched our temple work from the pews
baptismal font of alabaster oxen
chlorinated man and girl, their holy burden.
Water lapping shallowly at our temple whites, we prayed for the dead.

If I hadn't been razed through familial discord
I wouldn't feel so deeply the displacement of others
wouldn't see the government-broken people scooped up by missionaries
sent by churches, paid by governments

to displace people, break spirits,
pay churches to tell them they're whole
exactly what a mixed girl
who has been called "half" all her life
wants to hear.

Amen
I go under,
and again
in the name of Jesus Christ
my fortune slightly changed
Amen

2.
I don't know much
but I know how I got here

The first time I took the Expo Line
rounding the tracks, the sky opened suddenly
revealing the ancient yawning maw of mountains
and my first thought was that my grandma had seen this first
from a prison.

I took a risk on a whisper
followed an invisible thread to a
Vancouver full of ghosts.

A specter under the sign
driving past Slocan Street;

stomach of cold dread at the PNE livestock barn
buzzing cattle
cotton-candy shrieking, and smell.

Eighty years of burial and loss

I press bruises to see if they've healed.

3.

In my grief outside the hospital, the star magnolias
hang from their branches in the streetlights
like so many latex gloves
discarded.
I can't write much about our present past
I look at it in glances and overwrought words

My grandma lost everything but she still wrote that poem

I don't know much, but I know how to start again

with pine trees and wind
preserved in a poem
carried a lifetime
leading me here

Susan Kiyo Ito

• • • • • • • • • •

She Was Incarcerated/I Exist

If she and her family had stayed in her Western State
If she had remained in the house of her childhood
If her father (my grandfather) had kept his business
If her siblings had stayed in school
If they hadn't been taken by bus
  To the race track
If they hadn't gotten on the train
  With their single suitcases
If they hadn't ended up in the camp
  For three years
If they hadn't been released to the sponsorship
  Of a white church
  In a white town
far from the Western State
  Where she'd been born.

She might've grown up
  In her Nikkei community
  Finding a nice
  Japanese boy
  To date, marry, raise a family

But instead she grew up in the white town
  In a state with few Asians
  Nobody to date.
  Nobody to marry.
  Only white boys who wouldn't bring her home.

This is how I came to be
    Her mixed secret.
This is how she carried me
    Invisibly under her girdle
This is how she let me go
    In yet another state
This is how I found my Nisei parents
    Waiting over ten years for a Japanese baby.

If she hadn't been in that camp
    I wouldn't exist.

Dana Swensen

●●●●●●●●●●●●

Enough

The earthly was overrated, or maybe just all there was.

I couldn't help but feeling that her death had changed me

into an inheritor of the infinitely shelvable; objects which

my love for was outstripped only by my desire to arrange.

I became the tender of that which was left over after:

small kokeshi dolls, a set of wooden zori that Tokuichi

had carved in one of the desert camps, geisha figurines encased in glass,

red-lipped with faces of unfathomable, snow white.

And there was hardly any time for the abstract. The issues were

pressing but less a matter of our grief and more what to do

with the seven boxes of kimono that she had left behind.

I remember this as the time I saw my own face for the

first time in the faces of my great aunts but somehow lessened.

I remember going back to the house and looking in the mirror, touching the corners of my eyes and seeing myself as left over.

I remember seeing something that, whatever they told me,

did not seem to be a boy's face.

In any case, when I first imagined this poem I thought it would

include a dramatic scene in which we burned the kimono

on the beach while the sun set and we lamented the past.

But we just drove to a dump in Honolulu with the boxes

and threw them in with the other refuse of the island.

Shikata ga nai, uncle Nori said. But I didn't know enough to understand him.

Hikari Leilani Miya

Five of Cups

For my great-uncle
Kiyoshi Miya (October 15, 1917–April 29, 2007)

he saw spirits
his departed sisters
brothers
in his bedroom closet
so he slept
in his armchair
next to the patio
where his chocolate
lab Mochi
with her big hernia
guarded the farm
shop, those rusty
machines, copper
wires people stole
for cash

loaded shotgun
by his side
he went out
at any hour
if he heard
any disturbance
and shot
didn't matter who
was there, even if

no one was there he
drove his blue pickup
into the ditch

he called me Mary
didn't know
what to call
his dog, even though
I told him every time
I saw him sitting
in the shop with Mochi
panting by his side
radio on loud
he wasn't sure
he heard
but he'd always
say hello
how're you doing
I think this is
broken, can you help

so my grandmother
took him to
the place that was
supposed to help
where he climbed
over the fence
tried to find Mochi
his truck
his gun
until someone found
him, brought him
back in time
for dinner

the last time
I saw him

it was sunset
I was scared
to touch
his soft wrinkled
hands like prunes,
he couldn't
remember dinner
the president
his dog

mom said
he waited
until we came
so he could say
how're you doing
goodbye
and I cried underneath
the black grandness
of the piano

what I wished
I would have asked
him but couldn't
because I only learned
about 9066
while giving
his eulogy
saying things
my dad said
I should say

I would have asked
where did Baachan
bury your armor
the swords
the family crest
did she burn

them all
with her tears
before they were all
taken
to camp

the war
tell me
why you pledged
allegiance to a
nuclear bomb
dropping nation
why you served
what did you
miss the most
among those
bittersweet camp
memories

at ten years old
I didn't understand
passing, the priest
chanting in Japanese
saying we cannot
touch, speak
hear the dead

but I now understood
memory, how
the most frightening
battle
is with
your own
memory
your last
twenty-four hours
seen through

the eyes of
a dragonfly*

* There is a Buddhist story I was told at his funeral, where people bow to passing dragonflies, as they carry the spirits of the dead visiting loved ones for the last time.

Noriko Nakada

• • • • • • • • • • •

Nakada Issei / Translated into English / Means Lost in the Fields

Flee Okinawa's / smattering of rocky isles / overrun with pests.

Sail amber waves to / plant in America where / anything will grow.

Drop seeds so roots grow / native crops and fruits ripen / on this borrowed land.

Grow plants high enough / for the land to learn your name / and watch seedlings grow;

thrive in new fertile / soil. Surprise blasts from across / the sea rakes it all;

scatters family / across oceans, continents / Pacific, Europe

then into "camps" where / pale desert mountain prisons / keep watch over pests.

Stare at cold miles of / unsustainable dry plains. / No route for escape.

Now understanding / you are the pests, but plant seeds / anyway. Tend and

water crops again. / Watch new roots form; patiently / wait for lost seeds to arrive back home. But / witness your own withering. / Gone before lost roots

could grow, before any / seed, fruit or flower could bloom. / Gone before harvest.

Sharon Fujimoto-Johnson

Sand Island

In the year of fire, a man of small bones
walked its barbed wire rim. In a cupful of sand
he found conches so small they did not carry
the sound of waves. In my palm, they are the bones
of birds, against my ear, the voice of Sand Island
and my father's father whom I've never found.

Honouliuli Birds

Where the grass grows tall like mango trees
and the road to hell's valley is paved red with mud,
they filled a cage with birds and broke their wings.
In the shadow of kiawe bushes, the birds
raised their wounds to the salty wind.
But no one could recall why they were there.
When your mother's belly was not yet healed,
she carried you to the Ewa plains calling my name.
A bird thrashed in its chains and opened its beak.
I was once your father, you see. Once I could sing.
When she found me, I was a bird.

Patrick Shiroishi

● ● ● ● ● ● ● ● ● ● ● ●

Tori

whose sorrow do i sing about when the bluebirds are out?
is it okay that they are not mine but of my ancestors
two generations removed, their lives tucked into the soil

whose smiles do i flash when the hummingbirds are out?
their little wings fighting the air with everything
just like the thousands in the camps, their sons and daughters' lives
changed forever

whose tears do i shed when the sparrows are out?
do they stream down sandy faces dusted by the wind
or is it from the grandchildren of the camps, my brother and myself?

who's strength do i feel when the pelicans are out?
to dispel all feelings of hopelessness and anger and lament
i can answer my own damn prayers, i don't need to turn to the white
man who put you here

whose suffering do i feel when the swans are out?
tears watering tulips laid by the graves of fireflies
the suffocating cold when i stepped onto Tule Lake that sad spring
afternoon

whose love do i feel when the cranes are out?
filling me up to take on another day
to walk with love, to heal with love, to be with love

and to never forget.

what does the black crow see when i dream?

Micah Tasaka

●●●●●●●●●●

Tree (why my father didn't teach me Japanese)

a story:
the bomb fell in Hiroshima
but ricocheted across the Pacific
in Poston, AZ, it split a nerve
down the center of a tree
severing root from leaves

leaves deny their root
trees provide no shade
across a battlefield
war displaced a torn
ligament still spewing blood

blood sick with amnesia
across generations lost
roaming deserts for lifetimes
forget the language to tell
would rather not speak

speak about it no more
while in Nippon it rains
heavy heart from ceiling drips
dissolving tatami straws
falls through the floor

the floor cannot hold us up
we seep right through
in basement puddles

attempted rebuilding
a water forgotten molds

molds a thousand stories
unaware of ancestral tongues
still stinking of the dew
that forms on lips unused
performing a surgery

surgery, an art crafted from
these years of wondering
why we wandered so far,
might reconnect the veins
retrace the outline of a tree

a tree drawn on rice paper
cannot hold up to moisture
translucent to light, a fixture
pieced together, each leaf
remembers the feeling of branches

branches, a sound structure
we can only hope to assemble
what was never licked
by tongues that awkward form
the shape of a word

a word that shapes a feeling
burning inside of guts
when looking across a field
of trees still smoldering, questioning
why the match was ever dropped

Heather Nagami

The Gift

after Kenneth Tanemura's poem, "Japanese for Busy People"

And I hear myself in yours, Tanemura-san. A line of questions that fall into
a couplet that bleeds into the next

whispered answers, brief, temporary, your hush barely brushing the soft
hairs
in my ear, a hidden echo chamber

familiar to us. I never told you that my mother's father used to cry late at
night
after Camp. My aunt

would hear his sob seeping under her bedroom door. *I always thought it was
because he
couldn't speak to us, his own*

children, she told me. My mother said that he once took her to the movies
—James Dean and Natalie Wood. Even though he

could not understand, he sat with her, watched with her. Ken, I must confess
I did not know anata

before I read your poem, a gift of meaning, an understanding underneath
our correspondence
concerning authenticity,

our arguments about essentialism, deconstructionism. Exoticize,

Romanticize,
feminize—these are words we use

when we are not writing poetry, defining American standards of beauty as fascination with
the untouchable. To own

another language, an American vision of a foreign culture—an assurance
of American normality,

possibly, a fear of Japanese normality, maybe. One can only sustain an obsession by
keeping it packaged,

distant. The Japanaphiles, businessmen, the young white men who fetishize
me and other women of Japanese descent

mimic our teachers' lips like we do. They might form their words more
accurately than us. I can't help

but feel a camaraderie between myself and them. I cannot help but fear this.
I do not know

if their motives are more or less noble than mine. I do not know if that is a question
for me to answer. If we ever decide

why we search for answers within a language that is not ours,
the journey will come

to an end. We learn a language that we fear we'll forget out of lack of people
to share it with. A language

must be practiced daily to remember. My grandfather did not cry in words, but wails
known to anyone, as mourning,

though he practiced his language alone. I cry sometimes for his solitude, but softly.
His wails, resonating in my ears,

reunite with the breath escaping my lips. Another fleeting answer: we salvage
the phrases spoken

by ghosts, a resurrection that may end in rest. Natsu-yasumi
may sound awkward here

except for how you describe it—summer of rest. Tanemura-san is an address I use
not out of formality

but out of commonality. We yearn to hear each other, find each other, to make
our sounds
so heard

that even the dead will hear us speak.

Ali Meyers-Ohki

•••••••••••••

Invocation

They might have met anywhere. And they did. They met everywhere. In the Presidio as their families visited their imprisoned fathers. On the bus from the assembly center to the trains. In any number of lines—waiting for their barracks assignment, waiting to register with the school, waiting to buy a sewing kit at the camp store for their mothers.

Young queer love germinated, survived, dissolved, bloomed, quivered in camp.

They found each other. They spoke their own names aloud—as greeting, as introduction, as magic spell. They ran wild, gorgeous, leaping easily over repressed elders whose authority wilted limply against inflexible whiteness. Sudden closeness to many young people—also displaced, also disoriented, also lonely—stirred deep inside places, bloomed in the rosy flush of hot cheeks. Free floating atoms, they bonded. They had no language for the desire and resistance threading through their bodies. They only knew they had to hide. In shadows, they persisted, embraced, shoved, caressed, grabbed, entered, tasted, walked toward, walked away. They devastated. They liberated. They lived.

We have always been here. Shikata ga nai.

Spell Cast by Imagined Queer Ancestor at Amache

Dearest family, find your way to the floor. Let gravity embrace you. Surrender to the cradle of the earth.

Now, find your way to a beloved.

Hold them in your hand, or with your gaze, or with the limb of your mind.

Have you got them?

Good. Let the glow of your grasp be a talisman as we dive into the dark.

Somewhere, right now, an iron wisdom tooth is being extracted from its mountain mouth. It will be heated and cooled and squeezed into steel, cut and stretched into wire, woven into walls. Barbs will be sharpened.

The Ones for whom these cages are being made—they are already calling us. Can you hear them?

Somewhere, in a future that rhymes with here and now, there are closets meant for coats and unused furniture that are being painted and filled with interrogation chair, table, lamp. Inside, there are questions that are not questions and answers that are not answers. They pump in fog laced with hunger and fear and loneliness.

The Ones who will be forced inside—they already have our names in their mouths. Can you hear them?

Listen to their voices. Like you, they are the oceans. Like you, they are the flames and the dark damp earth. Like you, they are the unruly green and the decadent juice. They, too, have lost their belonging and their choice. Their pain is sharp. Their resilience is medicine.

We need them and they need us. Can you hear them?

Hold your beloved close. Feel for the warmth of the way you fit together and pass it through the spinning wheel of your heart. A spool of golden thread coils on the edge of your hip. Cast it out. And be ready to catch. These lines, they'll pull us all home someday.

Syd Westley

•••••••••

Elegy Attempts

I pick up my pen and put it back down again who died and what am I
trying to do

I have killed many plants I am notorious for overwatering

I am learning new words every day so I can say things that some people
have already known

If my grandmother's ashes are in an urn in Piedmont can I find my way
back and how so

Yesterday another trans woman died and I didn't cry until I couldn't
write a poem about it

There is a word for this in Japanese it does not translate I will not try

I drove seven hours north of Marin to confirm something my
grandmother once told me

The sky felt low and suffocating I thought I could not last two days here

How much violence does it take to make me a man I am hurting

After Pulse I did not write for many months I just did things I thought
were stupid like yoga

I am not a good child never was what was I saying

I was named after a man I did not know I am turning into him is this a
better elegy

When my mother wanted a girl I cut off my hair and left the house

There are memories that I will not write down will they die when I do I
really hope so

Can I write a poem about my grandmother without mentioning
internment once

There is no resurrection I have given her dresses to Goodwill

In the morning I will climb out of my bed and water my five plants how
insufferable can I get

She did not know I kissed girls would she have tried to leave the page

I press hard to the paper until my hand begins to hurt

Richard Hamasaki

• • • • • • • • • • • • •

Behind Barbed Wire

for Grandpa Senri and Grandma Yoshino Nao

Injustice provokes poetry
ruptures imprisoned memories

prolongs the will despite deprivation
laughing in its sleep, sullen even in pain

alone, withdrawn from its own bones' rhythm
groaning this evening, the tide too low for flight

Like shadows or a long and tender serpent's tongue
it reaches, picks rusted locks, opens gates

drifts through fences
beyond walls and barriers

tastes, then drinks
mutters and moans

finds humor even in poor company
humiliations lingering in its mind

Gazing at mountain peaks
reverberating with urgency

past censors, iron bars,
armed guards, through barbed wire

this ancient electricity heats the brain
with thoughts incarnadine

resurging family stories
of cunning artistry

of grandparents hiking through desert
finding then carving stone

grinding black ink with water
wet brushes touching paper

Mona Oikawa

●●●●●●●●●●

For Shizu

Assimilation.
This is the term of exile
from my Grandmother's
wisdom and strength.

I remember these qualities
from a childhood near to her,
hearing her voice:
lullabies sung in a language
grown foreign and faded.

It was her beauty
that was derided
by the white churchgoers,
the smiling white teachers
who told me to
drink milk and
pray to their god.

But never did they mention
her years of suffering in
the B.C. prison camps,
nor explain why she was
forever the enemy in
their renditions of World War II.

Learning their lessons well
I discarded that part of my spirit,

links to my Grandmother, my history.

Fleeing her image in the faces of the
Issei, Nisei, Sansei women
I might have known
and loved.

Now, as I discover the meaning of these memories
I want to tell her of their lies.
I long to swim across the years of difference
so silent and apart
to find safety once more in her arms.

Troy Osaki

●●●●●●●●

Minidoka is the First Camp Your Grandma is Incarcerated in, Crystal City is the Second

You thumb through your grandma's yearbook
    from when her middle school-self wore
whatever dress her mother could conjure.
    Maybe it belonged to a neighbor girl

from another barrack who grew out of it.
    Maybe it was unhemmed but fit well
enough. In camp, your grandma couldn't miss
    school without every other kid finding out

so instead, she missed her bedroom
    the daffodils off 14th near the temple,
how smooth Lake Washington was
    midsummer. She missed her dad

who looked like her but was taken
    elsewhere. In Germany, a grenade
goes off & your grandma is shoveled
    onto a train. Texas smells like pinewood

& sunburn. There's an unending fence
    similar to before. Your grandma is back
with both her parents & the war
    somehow feels a bit bearable.

The country you & her were born in

eventually wins & still she isn't
given back her dad's laughter, his morning
hum, all of what disappeared

for three years until her family was
imprisoned together. Decades after
your grandma is released she returns
to each camp her dad wrote to her from.

Montana Louisiana New Mexico Texas
The land is bare & whatever mess hall
or guard tower was once there isn't
as if the war is done, as if there isn't

a daughter left who's separated
from her dad. Somewhere a daughter
still is. If not in a camp, then at an airport
or behind a wall. Somewhere a dad

not your grandma's hasn't see the sun
in three days, hasn't breathed beyond
cement walls since before detainment.
& still your country says it won the war,

says it's proud of its name in its mouth.
You are in your grandma's home
as she bakes a sheet of sugar cookies.
Her memory becomes a kitchen knife

you hide beneath your pillow. You sharpen
its blade every night. You trust no country
that can smile & say its own name
with so much of someone else's blood

in its mouth. It's 1941 & you are at the center
of your grandma's camp. She's looking
at a mountain miles away. Says *sometimes*

I stand here, right here, staring & I swear

I can hear the other side.

W. Todd Kaneko

●●●●●●●●●●●

american sentences

During World War II, my father was imprisoned in America.
Seattle is far from Michigan, my father from my newborn son.
My father was a child back in that nowhere we call Minidoka.
Minidoka is a Dakota Sioux word meaning "spring of water."
My grandparents were captives too, animals stranded in the badlands.
Some call it relocation, internment; we just call it Idaho.
Before that, they lived in a little house near Seattle's Chinatown.
My Ji-chan worked all day, new gardens sprouting from beneath his huge thumbs.
My Ji-chan worked all night, night watchman pounding a beat through Chinatown.
My Ba-chan went to business college, kept books for Japanese grocers.
My father wasn't yet old enough to understand Minidoka.
Minidoka: family word meaning plume of dust, dirt in our mouths.
When the war broke, the soldiers shipped them all to the Assembly Center.
There, thousands of people waited on their way to the internment camps.
A sad irony: the Assembly Center was called Camp Harmony.
For months, they huddled in chicken coops, wept like piglets, slept like horses.
Camp Harmony was built at what is now the Washington State fairgrounds.
A sad irony: my father took me to the Washington State fair.
We fed the cows, then ate hamburgers on a bench just outside the barn.
He never explained how different the world looks from inside the cage.
Minidoka: that feeling in the animals' guts before slaughter.
When I take my son to the petting zoo, we do not talk about camp.

When I say camp, I mean Minidoka, where we lived without bodies.
I mean Minidoka, where our bodies lived without us inside them.
I was not at Minidoka, but I was bequeathed a piece at birth.
When we say sad irony, we mean Minidoka, still inside us.
I am shingle and tar paper, the sky's dry breath, at Minidoka.
I am barbed wire and fence post and coyote howl, at Minidoka.
I am the crow's bleak song, the National Anthem, at Minidoka.
My son is these things too, or will be when he learns of Minidoka.
After the war, my Ji-chan gave up the garden for a new death grip.
He broke birds by the neck, Minidoka in his hands until he died.
After he died, my Ba-chan lived in the darkest house in the city.
Neither of them ever talked to me about what Minidoka means.
After the war, my father carved out poems about Minidoka.
Poems about the cold desert, about how animals cry at night.
We never talked about what Minidoka means, but we have poems.
My father no longer survives with me on Earth, but we have poems.
Here in Michigan, my son will one day ask what Minidoka means.
One day, we will try to gather what Minidoka means together.
Together, our fingers might not be able to contain all of it.

Keiko Lane

●●●●●●●

Obasan's List

Always rinse rice twice, three times
if kids do it.

Make extra, even if there isn't any,
someone will always come.

If you watch plants, they grow.

Keep busy and they not notice, only
Kids will be one day nice to each other.

Pick only ripe ripe berries.
Customers like more better that way.

California ocean not same as Okinawa
different fish, different stories.

Clams sometimes look like rocks in moonlight.

Camp like sugar plantation, lot people,
not enough anything but sky.

Grandfather Explains

Whatever they told you is wrong.
It is not like they say.

It was no better anywhere. But was better
before war, everything is. Thought

it would be easier. We knew it hard everywhere,
but pineapples, sugar, different from Okinawa.

Marriage, supposed to, nothing else.
At least before camp there was someplace to be.

Yes. I read to them. Before your mother.
No. If they don't tell I won't.

The camp. Nothing to do but watch my boys climb
dusty trees. Barbed wire sky.

What else to do. Your auntie like
your mother. In hospital after camp then

she everything different but nothing change.
Wanted to leave but go where? My brother

left camp for Japan. Come back fifteen years later.
Honor where more? Strawberries then, after.

Why so many question? Spend life after forgetting.
Why you asking now? No need know.

No different from anything else. I don't remember.
Your mother. What she tell you? What she won't say

I won't. ? She told you

don't remember. She was the baby. Always drop
things talk too much. Too much noise. Had to

What could she know of before.
She come after. In camp. ?

Same as bent back, strawberries. Too much sound
like birds in dry brush at camp. You, nosy child

like your mother. You don't remember me?
Better that way for you.

Whatever they tell you is wrong.
It was much worse.

Rebecca A. Green

●●●●●●●●●●●●

Poston

For my mother

You were exiled to a land of desolation
coated with the bitter dust of hate.
Through barracks ripe with sweat and loss
the sea's receding fog moved day by day
as the forgotten coast paled in vision
and diminished like the tide.
The distant mountains suspended in heat
limned the momentous failure
of all that had come before this wire fence.
Your fury beat against the arid sun
until you became dry lightning
that struck the rustling ironwoods
and ridged lizards running free at dusk.
The rattlers coiled in silence wounded you
with slow poison to drain your captive rage
and flood the waiting earth with unspent life.
In the end you returned sundered by loneliness
and broken by your shame.
War's aftermath smoldered below as you tried in dreams
to outrun the desert sky that haunted you.
I wonder if injustice was replaced at last
with beauty unknown till then, profound enough
to overtop the violent stars in their fragile night
and if peace met you in your grave,
steeped in the coolness of release.

Paulette "Tkl' Un Yeik" Moreno

Daughter -" you were blooming "

mama, mama where has your soul went?
i asked as she slipped away…7 or 8 decades ago…
in moments she'd go to visit her child within
you know, the one with rice paper skin
and tlingit salmon berry lips

mama, mama "let's go together, i'm ready for the trip
i have 2 rolls of courage packed up like
seaweed for hunger and fuel for your body memories
"what hurts so much little mama……."
i want you to come back brilliant,
like big dipper stars and
shimmering northern lights

so we went to her place of scary race hate
we saw and spoke to the feelings
with big boots and wire hands that held her hostage
and we said, and i said, and we said
"NO MORE—unhand her, give her over, we are her people!"
and she floated back like raven wings and eagle down, softly landing…

and the good earth held her up and said "take her home"
and her drenched tear stained face,
cleared up like a cloud
being chased by the ocean,
away
and her spirit found
the salmon, halibut

and cod to play…
little Harriet is back and brilliantly unearthed
finally feisty like the courage we packed
in a seaweed wrapped package
oh Sacred Keeper of space
i see you clothed in leaves
as she walks up the shore
grey and white rocks
shells and pearls at her feet…

my mama, became my mother
as she renewed her ocean
of native abalone shine and the
japanese hues of blue herring grace,
by dropping that "unshed tear"
into the rim of the ocean's tea cups
and today mother and daughter play
"all along you were blooming"

Brian Komei Dempster

A Conversation with My Mother, Renko, About the Journey to and from Topaz Prison Camp in a Dream

A lotus is a lotus.
A train is a train.

No, this train is a lotus, this lotus is a train.

The petals are white swords.
The engine a head of steam.

No, petals are spumes of ash blooming from this train.

The bud opens to water.
The pistons drive with flame.

No, this train drives down the zone of the stem,
the petals fold back into a tunnel.

A lotus is a flower.

No, it is your cold body wrapped in cotton.
This bud is your lips muzzling milk
from your mother in the iron box.

A boxcar is a train.

No, your mother is this train, and her eyes are white cones
slicing mist in radiant columns. The boxcars slide
down the stem like drops of dark water.

You think I wanted to be this lotus,
I wanted to board this train?

No, the stem is not a lotus in mud.
You are buried knee-deep in a camp full of shit.
Your barrack is a box of panes and iron,
your camp a coal splitting with dust and plains.

The lotus may have been lost in the desert.
The desert may have been found in the train.

No, the train is a string of boxcars.
Each boxcar a chunk of dust I pluck from your stem.
Your stem is a mile of sharp, thistle wire.

I see a bulb sliding in you, my father.
Black steel ripping mist from tunnels. Your mother.
Steam and heat cleanse the walls. This is your lover.
A boy dripping with water is me, the son.

Mother, maybe steel thorns are milk, areolas rims
of light, the granite peak a triangle of hair,

. . .this soot is a flower,
your lungs a wisp of cinders,
your hair silver rail, your spine a track. . .

. . .veins are barracks, your knuckles
tar paper, this tower your throat,
this lotus your fist. . .

. . .your breast is my mouth, my tongue milk
your fingers white swords,

this stem your breath, it grew from flesh and dirt…

A lotus might not be a lotus.
A train might not be a train.

David Mura

• • • • • • • •

An Argument: On 1942

for my mother

Near Rose's Chop Suey and Jinosuke's grocery,
the temple where incense hovered and inspired
dense evening chants (prayers for Buddha's mercy,
colorless and deep), that day he was fired...

—No, no, no, she tells me. Why bring it back?
The camps are over. (Also overly dramatic.)
Forget *shoyu*-stained *furoshiki, mochi* on a stick:
You're like a terrier, David, gnawing a bone, an old, old trick...

Mostly we were bored. Women cooked and sewed,
men played blackjack, dug gardens, a *benjo.*
Who noticed barbed wire, guards in the towers?
We were children, hunting stones, birds, wild flowers.

Yes, Mother hid tins of *tsukemono* and eel
beneath the bed. And when the last was peeled,
clamped tight her lips, growing thinner and thinner.
But cancer not the camps made her throat blacker

...And she didn't die then... after the war, in St. Paul,
you weren't even born. Oh I know, I know, it's all
part of your job, your way, but why can't you glean
how far we've come, how much I can't recall—

David, it was so long ago—how useless it seems...

Steve Fujimura

• • • • • • • • • • •

From Sam

my mother listened at the kitchen table while Sam
her brother-in-law spoke about his back pain due to the
removal of two vertebrae which reduced his height by
three inches and almost no medication helped and he
wanted to shoot himself he said until he purchased
cannabis cream from a San Jose dispensary he can walk now but his
face looked sallow that Christmas Day in his Gilroy
home where my mother's side of the family gathered
I was glad Sam found some relief and
somehow we segued into talking about the
camps he said he was six years old when he went to
camp he remembered it was hot and he had to walk far
to the latrine or restroom and there was sand everywhere
in their barracks in their food in the mess hall he remembered
crunching his teeth on sand
and he repeated again and again how hot it was in the
Arizona desert at Poston where his father met my mother's
father on trips outside of camp to work in
agricultural fields during the day for the government for little pay
years later my mom's sister Chiyeko and Sam would
get married and Sam remembered how virulent
the racism was immediately after the war in Gilroy recalling
how a white man called Sam's father a dirty Jap in a
dry goods store and told the father in front of the son to
get the fuck out and Sam stopped going to that store
with his father which had to be humiliating
I asked if his parents
ever spoke about the camps they didn't and I asked

if he knew how they felt about going to camp and Sam's
eyes widened he said how do you think they felt how
would you feel if your entire family had to go there a prison and I
didn't feel it at first although I could certainly acknowledge
his pain intellectually until a few days later when I retold
the story to someone else and I began to cry I later imagined Sam
and Chiyeko and their kids my cousins who I've known all
my life forced to get on a train to go to the desert because
that's how it would have been for someone my age my generation
to be rounded up and put in concentration
camps today as Trump would suggest it with his
willfully ignorant followers
all of us punished for being
illegal due to gender skin color sexual orientation and class careful
not to persecute those who are poor and white and male today a Black
man yelling
at Berkeley police is forced into a
squad van and off to jail while a homeless white man is given all
the time and patience to rant and yell and move freely within a circle
of the same white officers
we saw this from the coffee shop
my coworkers who were brown and white and me
we wanted to take our cellphones and record
the Black man being arrested
because those white men could not tolerate him
a threat to their white masculine authority which
operated vehemently in the 1950s when Sam was a young man
in Gilroy working on the farm a sharecropper like my
grandfather and my mother picking strawberries all
day in the sun
my mother would later turn to books and movies
as a result of her father who purchased the newspaper in Japanese
who took her and her siblings to watch Japanese films in
San Jose and elsewhere along that circuit

a sea or field of

as my mom quietly listened to Sam and me
talking at the table Sam's experience attracted other
listeners such
as my aunt Nancy in the front room and Sam's daughter Barbara who
walked past
several times and I wondered if Sam meant to emphasize near Barbara
how hard he worked in those early days
raised a family with two jobs bought a house with barely enough money
he said his children never believed how hard things were
Sam is 80 now and while talking for two hours about his life
the color returned to his face
he did not want to be filmed or recorded
after all these years
he did not want to say anything wrong

Amanda Mei Kim

• • • • • • • • • • • • •

Wind structures, 1–5

1.

We pushed small spoonfuls of carrots and peas around to make our plates look more full. The caterers had run out of yasaimono.

–They'll remember to order more next year.
–Is this what camp was like?
–We don't know. We don't remember that.

–What do you remember?

–We were too young to remember anything. He was just a baby. His father had been taken by the FBI, so it was just his mom and his four brothers.

–That must have been so hard on her!

Their square jaws set into small smiles. The elven eyes of this white-haired couple dim for a moment. I could have kept my mouth shut.

–I remember the sand blowing hard and my father pulled a jacket over my head and carried me to the next building.
–I remember that too.
–That's all we remember.

In the black-curtained banquet hall, our white tables gleam with an inbound light.

–So, are you coming back next year?

–Of course!

2.

Aunt: The Buddhist school teacher would tap the blackboard with his chalk and tell us, *You are no greater, no bigger, no more important, than this tiny speck.*
Uncle: You are infinitesimal.
Aunt: You are nothing in an even greater nothingness.
Uncle: Even how much I love my boys, I know they are no more than a grain of sand.
Aunt: We are smaller than the smallest mark on the blackboard. Do you understand that?

In a way.

Aunt: In a way?! This is why it is so hard for us to talk to you.

3.

"In camp," people say. As thin as tissue paper, these words bag up and hold all the jangly word-knives of "temporary holding facilities," "indefinite leave," "native-born foreigners," "permanent resettlement," "war relocation as a service." Many replied with a potent silence that filled homes with innumerable projects of immeasurable complexity or drenched the earth with rage. Their silences arced like lightning around us. We, their children, meet them in their infinite refusal.

4.

Time and memory bend in the Mojave desert. This is where the state's oldest rocks and the world's oldest trees can be found, where indigenous people fight for water that was stolen 100 years ago.

My aunt and I each place a million-year-old pebble on the base of the I-rei-to. One for her mother who died in childbirth. One for the sibling who went with her.

"They said they could try to save the baby, but my father said, 'let them go.'"

Above the tower, the skies swirl with lakebed dust and particles uplifted from a landscape of strip mines, blast sites, open pits, bored holes and pickaxe mines. A drift of toxins sweeps over us and the multitudes who live in the desert crust.

We have come again, to a place where the rattlers and red racers meet, to water our memories.

5.

I told my aunt and uncle of the couple who remembered their fathers carrying them across the desert as toddlers.

–I remember that.
–Me too.

Here is the memory again:

–There was a terrible sandstorm, so my father picked me up and wrapped his coat around me and carried me to the mess hall.

–My father pulled my hat over my ears so they would not fill with dust and took me to the benjo. He had to wait outside in the storm while I went.

–The winds were so sharp that I couldn't open my eyes. My father carried me.

–We'd get knocked over, it blew so hard. Our fathers had to carry us to school.

In this memory, a familiar enemy could be contained by the individual strength of their fathers.

It was a psychic talisman that protected them as they moved from barracks to trailers to migrant labor camps to segregated schools and sundown towns. Other memories lost their purpose and disappeared, but this one is as durable as their bones.

IV
I Can Hold My Breath for Years

● ● ● ● ● ● ● ● ● ● ● ●

I can hold my breath for years,
Still my voice is strong and clear.
I dare you to hear me.

—**Miya Folick**, "Song for Kanjitsu"

traci kato-kiriyama

fire, near fire

Whenever we talk
In community
About Manzanar,
Or Tule, or
Internment, or
American
Concentration
Camps,
We often hear
About the dust,
The irrigation by
The hands of the
Japanese farmer,
The bitter winds,
The dances and
bands,
soldiers and
baseball.
We discuss
So little on the
Factions and
Fights between the
Incarcerees and those
They called
Dogs
For turning inward to
Police their own
Or the

Resistance behind the
Riots and the bullets that
Hooked in to the
Runners who tried
To pass over barbed wire hurdles
Or
The old men losing
their minds and monthly earnings
in gambling circles from
one Block to the next
Or
The queer lovers, hiding
Or
The queer lovers, contributing
Or
The queer lovers, loving
Or
The girls, who
Screamed and winced,
Naked,
Outside
Of a thousand eyes
From the stockade at Tule Lake.
We
Never
Speak much enough or at all
About
The
Fire.

Brittany Arita

• • • • • • • • • •

On Rage

where do i put it—the rage?
sharply angled & quiet

it is in the breath
faint & sour

at least with teeth
it may bite
breach skin & become

but breath is clear
almost silent
you can't hold it
fold & put it away

it must be exhaled,
released; spoken

but how do you speak
a story you haven't been told

Alison Lubar

• • • • • • • • •

For the No-Nos

Tule Lake Relocation Center, 1943

To the tar-paper shacks, no
one could live there. Did they know
this was prison? Crickets begin a soprano
chorus, each sottovoce *pian piano.*
Each note as pentatonic domino
cascades over the Monte Casino
growing along the fence. Sterno
distributed monthly, each inferno
rekindles what's lost: grannie's kimono,
the house, a hundred pounds. Cyano
sky. Peace always before the volcano.
Every body is a composite of amino
acids, chemicals. Atomic eternity. No-
thing else persists. No-
minal freedom. No
destiny manifest. No-
where. Hydrogen. No
body. Bomb. No
more.

. . .

Miya Iwataki

•••••••••

GAMBARE!

The 1981 President's Commission on Wartime Relocation and Internment of Civilians (CWRIC) heard over 177 testimonies on the Japanese American concentration camp experience. It was life-changing: for those courageous Issei and Nisei who broke a 40-year silence of anger, shame and gaman; for Sansei activists who fought for Hearings in more cities and recruited testifiers; and for our community whose fighting spirit was ignited by these stories, building unity and winning Redress. Their stories put a human face on the concentration camp experience, and educated an entire generation of Sansei. It changed my life. After the last day of Hearings in LA, churning with emotions from these searing testimonies, this poem erupted—with direct quotes and burning memories from stories that still pierce my soul.

1

THE STING OF EVACUATION
PIERCES THE COZY UNITY
OF THE TERMINAL ISLAND COMMUNITY.
48 HOURS
TO PACK 48 YEARS
OF LIFE.
FATHERS FIRST!!

"TO TAKE CARE
OF HER HUSBAND'S AFFAIRS
WAS JUST TOO OVERWHELMING...
SO SHE JUST SAT DOWN AND CRIED."

CRY, TERMINAL ISLAND WOMAN, CRY.

YOUR TIME WILL COME.

CURFEWS ON DISTANCE AND TIME
CARPETBAGGERS RIPPING OFF YOUR LAST DIME
NO ONE GAVE YOU A CHANCE
STEALING YOUR LIFE
FOR A SONG AND A DANCE.

CRY, TERMINAL ISLAND WOMAN, CRY.
YOUR TIME WILL COME.

2

IN THE DEAD OF NIGHT
SILENT BUSES STEAL INNOCENT FAMILIES
        AND UNSUSPECTING CHILDREN
TOWARD BARREN AND DESOLATE DESTINATIONS.
WITH SHADES DISCREETLY DRAWN
        SHROUDING PASSENGER WINDOWS
SO AS NOT TO OFFEND THE SENSIBILITIES
        OF SLEEPING WHITE CITIZENS.

ENDLESS CLOUDS OF DUST
A WHIRLING DERVISH OF ESCAPED DREAMS
        SLIPPING THROUGH FLOORS CRACKED
        UNDER THE BURDEN OF BROKEN HEARTS
AND SEEPING INTO WEEPING BARRACKS
SECRET STOREHOUSES OF STOLEN LIVES.

AND GUARDS, EVERYWHERE, GUARDS
TO PROTECT US FROM THE HOSTILE
                        WHITE
                        CITIZENRY.

BUT WAIT! LOOK!
GUNS POINTED <u>AT</u> US!
WAIT! NO! NO!!!
HIROSHI-SAN!

Hiroshi-san (whisper)
MY BROTHER
THEY KILLED MY BROTHER.

CRY, TERMINAL ISLAND WOMAN
YOUR LAMENT RINGS FROM
MANZANAR
POSTON
GILA
HEART MOUNTAIN
TOPAZ
MINIDOKA
TULE LAKE
JEROME
ROHWER
AMACHE
CRY, MY PEOPLE
THEN CRY NO MORE.
<u>OUR</u> TIME HAS COME.

3

THE IRANIAN HOSTAGES ARE HOME!
YELLOW RIBBONS FLUTTERING AMIDST PARADES
OF HAPPINESS AND PATRIOTISM.
YELLOW RIBBONS FLYING HIGH AMIDST WAVES
OF NATIONAL UNITY AND LOVE.

THE JAP-ANESE HOSTAGES ARE HOME!
YELLOW BANNERS WAVING GREETINGS OF
HATRED, HOSTILITY, AND BLAME.

THE HEROIC 442nd BATTALION IS HOME!
NO BANNERS, JUST SILENCE
TO COVER RACISM AND HIDDEN SHAME.

NO WORK, NO MONEY, NO HOME
NO JAPS ALLOWED!!

4

TODAY A COMMISSION
SITS ON HIGH
EXPECTING THE EMISSION
OF A SIGH
REPRESENTING THE SUBMISSION
OF A SHY, SHY
LAID BACK COMMUNITY
WHICH, TO THEIR SURPRISE
STANDS TOGETHER IN UNITY
ONCE AGAIN ON THE RISE
ONCE AGAIN ON THE RISE.

HAYAKAWA, THAT HAS BEEN BANANA
SINGS, IN AMERIKAN, “OH SUSANNAH”
SAFELY HIDDEN IN CANA-
DUH…WHAT’S UP DOC?
PRESCRIBING HIGH DOSAGE SEMANTICS
TO CURE THE SPEWING OF TRUTH.

DANCE, CHIQUITA HAYAKAWA, DANCE
YOUR TIME HAS COME!

ONE BY ONE, WITH EMPATHY, SUPPORT, AND PRIDE
WE TOLD OUR STORY
IN SPITE OF THOSE WHO TRIED
TO CUT US OFF
CUT US SHORT
CUT US OUT
ONCE AGAIN IMPOSING LIMITS OF DISTANCE AND TIME
NOW INSTEAD OF 48 HOURS
TO PACK AWAY 48 YEARS
THEY GAVE US 5 MINUTES
TO PACK 4 YEARS OF INDIGNITIES

AND <u>**40**</u> YEARS OF PRIVATE HELLS
AND EXPECT US TO PUT UP WITH OLD LADY
DYED HAIR, FOUL-MOUTHED RACISTS?!
OUR PEOPLE SPOKE LOUDER STILL!
PRESIDENTIAL APOLOGIES WON'T PAY MY BILL!!

ONE BY ONE, WITH EMPATHY, SUPPORT AND PRIDE
FILLING THE HEARING ROOM
SPILLING OUT INTO THE HALLS
WILLING EACH OTHER THE STRENGTH TO GO ON

WELLING UP WITH ANGER, AND
SWELLING WITH PRIDE
AS ISSEI AND NISEI STOOD UP AND TESTIFIED
TESTIFIED
TESTIFIED.
BREAKING LANGUAGE BARRIERS
TAKING PAINFUL MEMORIES OUT OF A DUSTY PAST
RIDDEN WITH HORSE STALLS AND TAR PAPER
SHACKS.
BREAKING A 40-YEAR SILENCE
GUARDED BY BARBED WIRE AND GAMAN.

AS EACH TESTIMONY SEARED MY HEART
SILENTLY SHOUTING
<u>GAMBARE</u>! DON'T GIVE UP THE STRUGGLE!!
AND I THINK THEY HEARD.

ONE BY ONE, WITH EMPATHY, SUPPORT AND PRIDE
SPIRITUALLY, EACH AT THE OTHER'S SIDE
ISSEI, NISEI, SANSEI TESTIFIED
TESTIFIED
TESTIFIED.
AS JAPANESE AMERICANS WE STOOD TALL

FOR JUSTICE NOW! REPARATIONS FOR ALL!
GAMBARE!

traci kato-kiriyama

No Redress

dedicated to ALL the ancestors who died before knowing that Redress & Reparations would be a thing to come or to be fought for in the future we call now

no museum

no monument

no poem
no song
can house
the spirit
of a passed soul
like that of my
grandfather
who died before
justice
could meet
the old man
at his mailbox

Grandpa
never got to
stand in line
at the bank
three inches
taller

with Redress check
in hand
one foot in front
of the other
feeling
grounded again

never got to deposit
an apology
in
his savings account

never got to wonder
of how he might
spend
this money
on new equipment
for the nursery or
a truck for himself or
college money for
his grandchildren
or
for once
take
the most
takai cuts
from the fish truck man

most years
in April

I attend
Pilgrimage

I say
Hello, Manzanar

I bow at the graves

I speak to the wind
of my hopes
for
Afterlife
to be a real thing

not so I can see
Grandpa again

but for him
to look around today, jump
into the circle, dance
the Tanko Bushi
and watch
me get it right

and see our friends
all our relations
learn what we mean by
chosen family
we are here

not only to remember

but to remind the local docents
this place will never
be a museum

this body will never
forget

and we leave Pilgrimage
with pledges as concrete
as the monument

we sing songs
to keep each other awake
on the long ride home

we lose sight quickly
rearview mirrors
a pitch black sky

where they close the gate
at the hour
they have had enough of us

where we leave behind
parts of our
best poetry

where I hope not
but
think
grandpa
sits
still
waiting

Noriko Nakada

●●●●●●●●●●●

Recalling Reparations

Dad's memory fails him now
so he cannot tell me
the number of days he was incarcerated
as a young boy in the desert.

He cannot remember what he bought
with the government check meant to repair
all that was lost, but he knows they did not count
the years stripped from his father's life.

He knows Okinawans have the longest life expectancy
unless you count the ones who died in caves
unless you count the diaspora
of ancestors scattered across the globe.

As his age swells into the nineties,
he can't remember if he paid taxes on those reparations,
but he knows he wants nothing to do with
family separations, or children locked up in cold cages.

He knows about the truth and forgiveness.
He knows something can be done to repair wrongs,
but no amount can be paid
that will mend lives ripped from home.

Syd Westley

●●●●●●●●●

Gender of the Day: Silicon Valley

My mother the capitalist
        says things are changing and
I am going to have to learn
        how to keep up with the times.
The skyline tells me there are buildings now
        much larger than our capacities
to run them. My grandmother
        tells me there is a shopping center
where Tanforan used to be,
        meaning there is no longer dust
or horse stalls or a small girl
        ruining her shoes in the mud,
and I don't mind.
        A shopping center is more bearable
than a concentration camp,
        I think. The point is that you
never owned anything that would stay
        yours, anyway.
Across a body of water
        I am in the place that birthed
gentrification. Across this body,
        I draw new lines everyday
to remember how I fit in
        to different spaces. Today
I wear purple satin pants because
        I am far from my family,
and across a body of water,
        they dream of all the dresses

I have hidden underneath my bed.
        I know things are changing.
I change them every day.
        A new body arrives, and
I send the last one back
        bored. I have been asked
how a trans person can live
        without grief, and I laugh
and ask how anyone can.

Angela Marian May

It's a funny feeling

A strange air is settling down on Powell Street
Down Jackson and East along Hastings, with no thought.
I stare in disbelief. I don't understand.

On the door of this place a sign has been posted by the City Health
Department. It says
CITY OF VANCOUVER
DEVELOPMENT, BUILDINGS AND LICENSING
REGISTERED AND REGULAR MAIL
LEGAL NOTICE
Dear Sir/Madam:
Cease occupancy of this building

ORDER TO VACATE
rooming houses like this,
real old ones,
not too well looked after;
run down and dilapidated and everything else,
holding any manner of things
Yu to yaroka?
burnt out tin cans and cardboard cartons and boxes and newspapers and
rubbish
serious wood rot
Running water on surfaces of walls
Visible mold in many locations
drywall soft to the touch;
Floors sagging
on-going concerns

What do you expect?
a landscape made up relatively small, densely packed residential units
deteriorated after their inhabitants were taken from them
bought up by people eager to take advantage of a bargain.

the buildings speak to those who will listen.
It's like a roar, a steady roar.

I stand transfixed
Rough-looking white guys, and sometimes women
the junk man on Alexander Street
the *ganbari-yas*
the *itazura,* the *yancha*
can't stay in this rooming house any longer.
It's just what the hell, why should they have to go anywhere?

LEGAL NOTICE
ORDER TO VACATE
Later when no one's looking I tear down that sign

What am I doing? Who cares?
But I don't like what I'm saying, and
I don't know why, but I do remember
on the far side of Powell grounds, under the big chestnut trees
a whole crowd
just hanging around together
approximately 50 Regent tenants
that swagger of the fishermen
I can't recognize any but I wave and wave
They wave back and I can see that some of them
are shouting.

it's said
that the building has been condemned because its unfit for human
    habitation
The City of Vancouver's chief building official has determined that,

everybody, but everybody, is going to be moved out.
I don't know. But I think so.

I am throwing up until I can throw up nothing but
parts of the body
I wonder what
the hell's going on,
I wonder about my wonderment, and remember
decades of underinvestment and mismanagement
previous City Orders
people, men scurrying about from doorway to doorway,
or going through the myriad of little passageways
corridor walls
between houses and buildings along Powell Street.
mama:
Kakugo wo suru, she says, brace yourself for the future

I have thrown up
I don't know how many times, and
heaved myself inside out.

this community
also undergoing a dispossession
we have a deep connection

It's a funny feeling.
It's quiet now and I am going to fall asleep.*

* Author's Note: This is a found poem. It uses four sources. Two are focused on the Japanese Canadian community, and two are focused on the Downtown Eastside community. Both communities share the Powell Street neighborhood as a historic (Japanese Canadian) or present-day (Downtown Eastside) home. The sources are: (1) Jesse Nishihata, *Powell Street Diary* (Lulu Press, 2017); (2) Audrey Kobayashi's *Memories of Our Past: A Brief History and Walking Tour of Powell Street* (Vancouver: NRC Pub, 1992); (3) the legal notice of closure posted on the Balmoral Hotel on June 1, 2017, (4) a press release about the closure of the Regent Hotel dated June 20, 2018.

James Fujinami Moore

notes on the phrase shikata ga nai, written after a Colorado state representative says in 2017 that the internment camps were justified because "in the heat of battle there isn't time to distinguish who is a citizen and who is not," or: it cannot be helped

I am so tired of talking about Manzanar.
Lord, let me talk about anything
else instead. The moon, the sea, even fucking flowers
I'd rather write than these desert stories muled as a kid,
old as black bile, a myth, America,
of your forgiveness, of what couldn't be helped.

That phrase in rōmaji, *it cannot be helped*
engraved on stones they sell at the gift shops in Manzanar
alongside baseballs, tiddlywinks, tin American
planes with their tin tiny bombs, anything
a souvenir, a replica poster for the kids
saying where to go, hiding behind the "Japanese-style" flower

vase on sale. Some days I say history and mean ikebana.
Sometimes bonsai. Question: with sharp enough clippers, can you help
any tree grow small? With sharp enough clippers, can you outlive your
kids?
A tree is a reflection. In the bark, ōoji's unendurable face. Before

    Manzanar,
there were strawberries. After, there were also strawberries. Anything
can be celebrated with strawberries in America,

your fields promising red on your lips, your teeth. America,
I still whisper this poem. In your heart even the sakura
blooms for your old dead soldiers, everything
pink, everything brief. The Paiute lived here before Manzanar,
were removed,   and returned,   and helped
build too. You conscripted our dying to dig our graves. Each boy

giving their mute answer to the guards, each boy
saying *yes*   saying   *no*   *no*. Our traitors
fought for you, America. They just wanted to go home.
Where I'm from there's no cherry trees, just dead wisteria
washed in drought. At Manzanar
I was a garden, I was a maid, I sold groceries, bled rabbits, all

blooms with a spade. I was your issei, your nisei, your sansei
I was your viper-hatched son.
Question: *Hast thou gods before me? When have you prayed?*
According to your survey, my Americanness is irrational.
They say you planted victory gardens
in our absence. They say you'll let us return.

Great-uncle says the suffering helped, America.
He gave his kids his citizen pride. Today only flowers
bloom over his grave. He went blind too, after Manzanar.

Troy Osaki

•••••••

My Grandparents Plant a Pear Tree in the Backyard of their Home in Northeast Portland

When my grandpa asks,

Say, how many jars do you think we have left,

my grandma replies,

Gosh, at least six or seven.

They offer me a pint of slices

they canned months before.

Tell me how canned pears last years

beyond expected. I trust what they know

about preservation is air-tight.

When the season is kind

they gather a bundle of barrel-shaped fruit,

bury a handful of wedges

beneath two splashes of water,

then sprinkle in sugar

before sealing them snug. I'm not surprised

my grandparents know preservation

like a past life, like they've practiced

for centuries now. For as long

as I've known them they've kept this family

alive. Once, before tending to a backyard

full of fruit, my grandpa was a school teacher.

In his first interview, he was told,

The school board chairman doesn't like Japs.

& rather than let the corners of his body bruise

like a rotting peel he replied,

Is that right you say? He doesn't like Japs?

Well then… I'll take the job!

Before that my grandma was snatched

from her family's grove, boxed away

in a warehouse made of barbed wire.

She found sugar in whatever wicked shelf

America shoved her in. & still

when the war ended it didn't disappear.

Years later, in a schoolhouse hallway,

a boy who smelled of famine yelled,

You must be mad because your country lost!

& I don't know if any word has been invented

for that kind of patience—to soothe a rage

that would burn 1,000 acres of orchard

if given the chance. Maybe *miracle*

is the closest I can think of.

Maybe my grandparents are so good

at not giving up they gain another life

whenever someone fails to poison

the patch of soil they breathe on.

Maybe in a past life, they were blooming pears

that outlived the coldest winter.

Michael Prior

•••••••••

The Border

It's night. I'm not from here. Inside
I'll press my fingers against the screen,
recite my monosyllabic fealties
while their dog sniffs up and down my leg.
I won't be who they're looking for.
Once, my grandparents were. A suitcase each,
they shuffled down chain-link corridors
and slept in livestock stalls. He was twelve.
She was eight. Their lives incised
by a hyphen that hadn't held, a censor's
smear of ink. I think of how the dappled dark
holds all other nights, like the faces in a face.
Of how this falling snow is a kind of sleep.
Of countries dreaming of being awake.

Sesshu Foster

• • • • • • • • • •

Visitation

1.
the desert sky obvious: clean
and clear above the owens valley.
the disparate cottonwoods reach
down through percolating soil, lean
into space in their wait
for the melt or infrequent rain,
leaves fluttering greenly
in today's breeze. in august
or september cotton may drift
over the gravel.
at manzanar
there's a graveyard for those
permanently relocated
'for their own protection' and a stone
marker erected after the fact.
you deviate from 395,
you leave footprints before
the winter winds. beyond
the car there's no electric cord
to hold, plug you into their rage
forgotten or forbidden, out of all
practically placed behind them now.
just this mark enroute
lives took (unsung they remain
behind the billboards of popular
songs of daily broadcast) taking the silence
home

as cottonwoods take lightning
to ground,
crack, splinter
and burn. all winter
leafless, they're frozen under
the black clouds.
the people have gone,
they have turned back to
their work.

2.
those sleeping in the land
in the creosote bush and ashen dust
swirling around the big stones
are beckoning to you and you
are beckoning to them
with your memory

you remember the names
you read of the camp and the travelers,
what happened here when the ribcage
of home was finally pulled free
from the backbone of the spirit,
and the dates when the heart here
ended.

3.
they were needed for cheap labor,
but no way were they the only
ones, or even the first.
agribusiness required a constant surplus
with wages controlled: the mexicans
and chicanos deported, families split
by train when the war ended.
oakies and arkies had been absorbed
by the growth of the military-industrial plant.
chained to trees and blowtorched

in poverty the oppression of rural blacks
an exodus to the inner city,
labor reserves. the chinese had been hounded
off the land into picturesque ghettos
for piecework in local sweatshops.
indians, hindus, mexicans, and white people, too,
in the fields, and filipino men (men
alone) stooped beside them.
the short-handled hoe. native americans corralled
far out on the land in houses like dog houses
while stray dogs starved. who spent
those years imprisoned for who they were?
who drove the bullet-nosed chevy
parked outside the TV home?
who had the cushy job, wife at home
getting anxious about the uppity
teenagers?
did the g.i. bill of a generation
whose parents would've voted for roosevelt
stop them from asking whose interests the state
reflects?
who benefited?
in the rows of strawberries, spinach and spruce vegetables
it was human beings,
this time japanese,
who were made
redundant.

4.
PASSPORT FOR THOSE WHOSE IDENTITY
HAS BEEN OFFICIALLY REMOVED

immigrant
through barbwire
child of the cold dawn,
your destiny runs in all directions
ice crystals forming in the ruts

where the puddles freeze over
(a sea of mud in the spring,
a plain of dust each summer)
the season turns on you and your
children,
the belongings proletarian, forsaken
by history, but not by
racists for their gain.
this was why they made the law.
asian exclusion act,
anti-miscegenation laws.
japanese could not own land.
these are not my words:
mere facts rising above ancestry.
what was done:
turn your back on the past,
it is theirs, their private property,
codified/coagulant in the lines
and scars on the maps of the skin.
face forward / face the future.
they will get the line of your jaw
along your shoulder.
that's good enough
for them.

5.
soldiers conducted the music of transport,
slow march to the dirge
sung on desert winds,
poston, arizona.
they'd say bureaucratic victims of "war
hysteria." lies: racism.
the only giddiness in the hatred
was in the shuffle and denial
of the cover-up.
(the soviets with their 20 million dead and humphrey's
bill to build new concentration camps for communists

for the cold war of u.s. hegemony
on top of the world, entering the space age)
while the shakuhachi note of issei sorrow
practically lost through the war,
though the war on fascism was won—
with blood in other
bloody homelands, but not won at home.

soldier's death in the distance brought
medals, paper, flowers, to rest on
little black and white photographs
of our faces and our people standing
against the wall, but the flowers
from la jornada del muerte blew atomic
petals across the dawns

6.
OKAY?
Based on a photograph by Dorothea Lange of a Nisei girl sitting on baggage before the departure

under that calm wing of black
hair your dark eyes watch
in wait, glance sharply above
the collar of the thick
winter coat you wear,
wool in may, since you must
carry everything yourself
now, and tag it with your
number

it was only a matter of years, mother,
before you freshened your face
in ordinary storefront windows.
it was only years, grandfather,
before you walked this sidewalk
stooped as if from strawberries

like any other american.
child, tagged like baggage,
your black eyes watched that
highway of silence

7.
jeff told billy and me,
"i never killed anybody,
i didn't put the indians on reservations,
i didn't take away their land.
i don't hate black people.
where i live there aren't any
black people. i didn't put no japanese
people in concentration camps.
i was only twelve when the vietnam
war ended. i didn't kill any babies.
it ain't my fault. besides,
all that shit is
over with."

billy said, "the thing that shocked me
most was when i heard that black people
could not be on the same baseball team.
that's what i remember most."

after the summer in colorado
spent fighting forest fires, jeff went back
to college in bemidji, billy went back
to the university in fort collins,
and i went to work
in seattle.

8.
the towers disappear from the brush,
the iron barbs oxidize in time
and drift into the sand.
the mountains still rise pink

in the sunrise above the site.
you can stand there yourself
to see,
you can stand anywhere you want
and still see.

Brynn Saito

●●●●●●●●

Theses on the Philosophy of History

Or: Listening to the Presidential Debate While Stuck in Traffic

1.
Roads clog with people in vehicles crossing the Golden Gate
Give my rage back to me, I know how to hold it
Ghost fog grows and stretches itself through the bars and I'm ready for it
On my radio, the white general and the white general
yank each other into the deep end, good heavens
Don't teach me to hate my language tonight
Don't teach me how to hate my lips and their language tonight
Tongo says capitalism walks on water, I've seen my TV, I believe it
All of the redwoods in the world can't keep this country from wanting to
    die
The future has arrived and it's doubled over
and the best of us are ready for love though we're burning

2.
Roads clog with people in vehicles crossing the Golden Gate
My family is Eduardo and Mitsuo and Marilyn and Alma
and Samuel and Fumio and the twin who drank himself to death
and the auntie who drank herself to death
and the Issei and the Nisei and the Sansei with their rock faces and
    nightmares
Undisguise me, said the stone
Undisguise me, said the stone to the desert light
Undisguise me, said the stone to the river
Lay me down under harsh water flowing under midnight starlight
Take my face off of my face, said the stone, shake me open

3.
Roads clog with people in vehicles crossing the Golden Gate
The white general and the white general
teach me how to hate my language on the radio tonight
Which nightmare of a framework makes the human count
Which bodies count and which count against
Grandma met Grandpa in those camps
Let me give your rage back to you, said the poem
Stop trying so damn hard, said the poem
Everything that has ever happened to you and your family
keeps happening and the love keeps coming in with its surgery
Get good with yourself, said the poem, get gone

Greer Nakadegawa-Lee

Plaything

If I kick you out of the stores.
If I spit on your name.
If I leave graffiti on your walls.
If I dismantle your face into propaganda,
If I force you to pack your life into garbage bags,
as if to show you just how much I value it,

will you bear it?
Will you still let me call you my children afterwards?

If I suffocate you in wire will you still fight my wars for me?
If I treat you like animals will you try to make your hands more human,
will you make crafts with them,
play baseball,
try to convince one another that things could be worse.

Does it bother you
that when I teach your grandchildren what I did to you,
I will use my calmest tone of voice.
I will emphasize the sound of running water,
of chuckling through the thin walls,
I will talk about what a stoic prisoner you were.

If I wind you up now,
do you still smile?
Do you still march around the room,
If I pick you up now do you still hang your arms limp.
Will you let me put your body on the operating table,
let me keep the parts of you I want to play with?

Steve Fujimura

• • • • • • • • • • •

Fred Korematsu Day, Jan 30

it's JA day
every day, no, well
for those
with this skin
these names
and this history

and if yours
aren't with you
every day, then
what is
with you

Michael Ishii

• • • • • • • • •

Tsuru For Solidarity

This poem was performed for the 2020 Day of Remembrance in collaboration with musical artist, Kishibashi as a call to action at the fences of the Northwest Detention Center where immigrant men and women are being incarcerated by ICE. Over 600 Japanese Americans turned out during a severe winter storm to stand in solidarity at the fences, hanging thousands of origami cranes. Tsuru for Solidarity is a national organization formed at the Tule Lake Pilgrimage in the summer of 2018 in protest of child and family detention.

If you seek an army for vengeance
you will not find it here

If retribution is the cry
We will not join you

When we employ violence against humans: physical, economic,
psychological, spiritual, sexual
If we violate children, the sacred trust

Then we act against ourselves and the universe

***

We are the crane people
fragile wings torn. bruised. resilient.
Born from righteous indignation

If you too search for courage to raise your voice and come to the fence in

solidarity
Armed with a faith in humanity
Then join us

***

From every corner of the community
prayers inscribed on their wings
Come tsuru
Los pajaritos de curación
Talismanic
Instilled with ancestral kimochi
Containers of long-held grief spilling forth
Kodomo no tame ni

Folded by hands that remember the sting of desert sand and wind
holding memories of gaman
Of horsestalls, guard towers, stockades, hardened resolve,
silent tears
Of surveillance, manipulation, questionnaires and fracturing
Of Obachan's despair
Of guards' hands defiling young bodies,
Of clenched fingers bearing weight of suitcases filled with anxieties

These hands remember intimately, fathers taken in the night, silent terror, forced removals, separation of families, children behind barbed wire
Into the wings of the tsuru are folded a thousand prayers
the thrum of taiko resonating the cries of humanity
and the resplendent light Amaterasu returned to the world
to force back darkness

But in this time, it was our own incarcerated children who remembered
We are the Tsuru
Bringing the light and resonance
Knowing rightly to return to the fences
engendering the wisdom to understand healing across time and space

Across oceans and divided countries
Opening the future

Tsuru, fly from Hiroshima
To Puyallup
To Minidoka, Manzanar, Heart Mountain, Granada, Rohwer, Jerome, Topaz, Poston, Gila River, Tule Lake…
And to Dilley, Laredo, Fort Sill, Yuba, Tacoma, Berks, Fort Bliss, Greensboro…

Tsuru, soar to those targeted for destruction
Pass thru barbed wire and chain link fence
Offer your preference to those most targeted
Alight with those starving themselves in resistance
with families torn asunder
fly to those despairing inside the cages

Join here to hold the center and look back directly at the violence
Itai, Itai…

Touch your wings to minds lost in torture of others
Bring your light to these desecrated places

We call upon our Ancestors
In time of greatest need
Help us fly home to one another with resolve
And to our furthest and most internal spaces
our luminous centers
Embracing strength, wisdom, kindness
so that in radiant constellation
we may return together to end the violent cycle of forced removal,
mass incarceration, separation of families, deportations
And together heal the wounds spanning across generations

Satsuki, Nancy, Bruce, Carl, Duncan, Tsuya, Joy, Lisa, Tom, Holly, Akemi, Kiyoshi, Emiko, Chizu, Masako, Lam, Jun, Nora, Maru, Leslie, Margie, Erin, Sparks, Deepa, Maya, Taryn, Julia, Rini, B.,

Silky, Kaoru, Stan, Bárbara, Shoshana, Nobuko, Suzanne, Keiko, Becca, Celeste, Katharine, Mika, JJ, K.C., Allie, Betsy, Roby, Yuri, Bill, Michi, Mineo, Gunzo, Misao, Denise, Tadashi…

sister, brother, neighbor, survivor, descendant, stranger, friend…

We are Tsuru for Solidarity

Erica H. Isomura

●●●●●●●●●●●

Haibun for February 19

After the Tsuru For Solidarity & Densho Day of Remembrance, Day of Action on February 23, 2020 at the Northwest Detention Centre in Tacoma, WA

We stand // huddled together // drenched // along barbed wire fence
strung with hundreds upon hundreds of origami cranes
such delicate paper frames // creased wings flap in the wind
clouds spinning

I never thought somebody could camouflage into a mass
of rainbow rain jackets // Each person arrived dressed in layers
as if destined for a Pacific Northwest trailhead

Instead // this protest not pilgrimage // led me to drive across the border
into Tulalip-Duwamish-Puyallup-territories

I find myself in Takhoma // named after a snowy white peak
which could have been more peaceful if not for the sheer ICE
detention centre

Confronting bad climate // a crowd chants

// *LIBERTAD! NO MURALLAS!* //

Hoping the people locked up inside know how much
we value their lives

On the mic a survivor dreams of marching on Washington DC
to close the camps and convene the largest gathering of Japanese
Americans since forcible removal from their homes
seventy years ago

ume blossom embraces
the tree branch—
seagull flies away

A JC cento, or why does silence become a shard?

I've been tracing the shape of my lifeline *Carolyn Nakagawa*
Through livestock-stalls and mud *Michael Prior*
Grown foreign and faded. *Mona Oikawa*
Persistent, persistent, echoing… *Laura Fukumoto*

All the years we've travelled separate ways *Roy K. Kiyooka*
How hungry we were! *Hiromi Goto*
An icy lemon kakigori pride
melting on my thirsty tongue *Rita Wong*

How come we have so little to say? *Roy K. Kiyooka*
We bury the ashes *Joy Kogawa*
Looking for stubborn, black swishy strands of *Rita Wong*
memories, river stones, *Prior*
I discarded that part of my spirit *Oikawa*
keeping my pack light, barely noticing the curve *Nakagawa*

How many ripples are made through time? *Fukumoto*
Alone we are helpless, but together a fury! *Goto*
Heart and feet beat in sync *Erica H. Isomura*
The aspiration to be! *Roy Miki*

What remains elusive is the sense of freedom I keep
thinking will come with nightfall *Angela May*
Illuminating nothing, everything *Isomura*

And if, and if *Kogawa*
I can't, won't be there for the rally,
for the wake, for the forgetting *shō yamagushiku*
Why prolong history? *Miki*

What comes is only stillness:
a row of gravestones made of miraculous mirrors

May
yamagushiku

Miya Folick

•••••••

Song for Kanjitsu

My words matter to me,
So I won't speak,
Till you see me as human.

My world matters to me,
So I will keep myself clean
Because I'm human.

Dust in the air is a knife in my throat,
But I keep waking up and hanging out the clothes,
Pinned up to dry,
Billowing on the line,
And so am I.

I can hold my breath for years,
Still my voice is strong and clear.
I dare you to hear me.*

---

* Author's Note: Densho asked me to compose and perform a song about my family heritage for their 25th Anniversary Gala. I procrastinated for a while, not knowing where to begin. But then my mom revealed a small detail about my grandfather Kanjitsu that gave me a path into the song. She told me this story, as she tends to do, in such a casual manner with the air of "didn't you know this already?" No, mom! I didn't know!

During WWII, my grandfather Kanjitsu was sent to prison before joining his family at Minidoka, because he was a Buddhist minister and community leader. I had known this for a while. But what I didn't know was that he performed a silent protest at the prison, refusing to speak. I wrote this song both about Kanjitsu and about my grandmother Kyoko, who was sent to Minidoka alone, pregnant, and with a small child.

V
Be Strong Now

● ● ● ● ●

Be strong now
Hand In hand
For within the stillness
You will see
The eyes of tomorrow today

—**Paulette "Tkl' Un Yeik" Moreno**, "Earth's Aging"

Starr Sumie Miyata

To My Ancestors, Forgive Me

I used to dream of breaking your silences, to
crack the world open like an egg
spill the yolk, this the balm to heal us.

today, I only dream of
cutting you apples.

ringlets of peel soft as cedar shavings in the sink as
the thick slices brown on your plate.

to sit at your feet, give small hands to
the stiff arches, thickened soles,

my head in your lap
the warmth of ourselves inseparable
the greatest gift, this quiet together.

Casey Hidekawa Lane/Levinski

Omiyage: Rituals

always, a plum
picked from the juice ripe branches
or a handful of crisp daisies
each carefully pulled from the earth
perhaps, a persimmon reveals itself
tucked in our pocket
foraged last winter and dried
an offering exhales into being
wildflowers wrapped in twine
apple turnovers
a handmade wooden box
just large enough
to fit a prayer and a handful of hard candies
zenith at the plum tree
when spring returns
to our doorstep
the windows yawn open
the persimmons
rotting in the kitchen
become an offering
for the worms and topsoil
we drink chrysanthemum tea
in the evenings and track
the phases of the moon

Ars Poetica

NEW MOON

At the precipice of archive
My epistolary childhood
I wrote diligently to reach my most beloved
Waiting to die from his recliner
My grandfather becomes an unveiled creature

WAXING

Entombed upon the sea
I have lost the exactitude
That constitutes a grave
But for his ghost
A ginger chew sticky against my molars

FULL MOON

The most auspicious of burials
A leveled desert
Where we waited to become American
A leveled desert
The most auspicious of burials

WANING

A ginger chew sticky against my molars
But for his ghost
That constitutes a grave
I have lost the exactitude
Entombed upon the sea

NEW MOON

My grandfather becomes an unveiled creature
Waiting to die from his recliner
I wrote diligently to reach my most beloved
My epistolary childhood
At the precipice of archive

Brian Komei Dempster

Topaz

I am the prism

refracting

your prison.

My ancestors,

the jewels

set in sand.

Through facets

I etch memory.

From crystal

my lines

are cut.

Paulette “Tkl′ Un Yeik” Moreno

Earth’s Aging

Together we pray for our families of our ancestor’s lands
May our Mothers be Comforted and our Fathers Strong
For Nature has taken her course
And with her has went many of the brown people of our skin
May our people’s children believe in eternal freedom
Our heart’s cry
Tears upwelled
For thousands toil the pain-stricken earth
Some have journeyed and some are still amongst us…
Deep within the skin of mother earth
Be strong now
Hand in hand
For our people have toiled the land
And created a nation from within their home
To take a stand!
The Pride!
My Brothers My Sisters
Be strong now
Hand In hand
For within the stillness
You will see
The eyes of tomorrow today
And today you will see
Our Children’s Earth Aging

Mia Ayumi Malhotra

To My Many Mothers, Issei and Nisei

Praise be to beef liver stew, to gravy biscuits
    and home-baked bread, to women
in work pants and suspenders who *worked like dogs*
    in the packing shed, up to elbows
in rose clippings. You fed us well, O goddesses
    of goulash and green beans, of Sunday dinners
wrangled from the coop. For penny money
    and seamstressing, praise. For parsnips
and sweet potatoes, praise. Even for the years lost
    to sharecropping and strawberries, hallelujah.
You worked until the final hour then rose
    three days later, baby squalling on your hip,
back to breaking canes, clipping hooks,
    hustling the men through lunch hour.
No breaks, boys. Hallelujah to Pond's Cold Cream,
    to curling rags and church bento socials.
Praise to the nursery truck revving in the morning,
    the clank of steel pipes and boiler-
house rumble. All glory to the Berkeley street car
    and Key Route electric train, the smokestacks
of Richmond and foggy peaks of San Francisco.
    And because they're what taught us to praise,
glory to the roses run wild, the packing shed
    left to cobweb. Praise to the crowded horse stalls
and half-built barracks of Rohwer, Arkansas,
    dusty sheets and muffled nights of Block 9-C-C,
100. Sakai, Chu. 102. Sakai, Ruby. 103. Sakai, Kazue.
    O praise to the camp midwives, the Nisei girls

shooting hoops and swatting birdies when their mothers
    weren't looking. And to the college-bound coed
who crossed the country, camp release papers
    in hand, hallelujah. Her truth marches on.

Carolyn Nakagawa

Tegami

...how come we have so little to say
given all the years we've travelled separate ways
—Roy K. Kiyooka

Since we met, a mirror is less like a tool
and more like a talisman. A small one
to hang on my neck, to rest on my heart.
I've been walking an arc of this wide circle,
keeping my pack light, barely noticing the curve.
I've been tracing the shape of my life line
and letting it leave my palm.

Let's give up on language so we can find it again,
sifted through memory and time's dust.
The things I can hold I will offer to you,
whether or not they are silent. A packet,
a morsel, a song. The past is your own map,
a route travelled grown strange. All these years,
we've known only separate ways. We have so much

and so little we need to say.
Write it anyway.*

---

* Author's Note: "Tegami," literally "hand paper," is the Japanese word for "letter." This poem was written as part of an invitation to other young Japanese Canadians to create poetry or other artworks from a shared prompt (the Kiyooka epigraph, selected by the author).

Lauren Emiko Ito

●●●●●●●●●●●●

Arrival As We

Thousands of women hum in my blood
Forced to play god
    Cradled their knives with a gentle hand
Lifted gazes to the horizon
And summoned air
Tucked it into laugh lines
A teacup
A birthmark
A prayer
For generations yet to unfurl
Knowing breath is never promised

Always
Especially these days

Always.

Always.

Remember this
Inhaling sunrise and birdsong

We never arrive alone.

Gratitude

The work of putting this anthology together was supported by grants from Colorado College and California State University, Fresno.

We want to express our love and gratitude to the people who accompanied, encouraged, supported, and inspired us, and who provided us with guidance and connections, throughout the making of this anthology: Frank Abe, Selfa Chew, Raul Contreras, Dot Devota, Lee Herrick, Lisa Lee Herrick, Karen Ishizuka, Dave Lehl, traci kato-kiriyama, Koji Lau-Ozawa, Alison Lewis at Frances Goldin Literary Agency, Ignacio López-Calvo, Mia Ayumi Malhotra, Nate Marshall, Nikiko Masumoto, Kirsten Emiko McAllister, Harumi Nako, Bao Phi, Michael Prior, Rajesh Ramakrishnan, Ruth Sasaki, Yumi Taguchi Schumaier Shimoda, Jennifer Shyue, Janine Sun, TT Takemoto, Natasha Varner, Patricia Wakida, shō yamagushiku, Kaori Flores Yonekura.

To Emily Peacock, for her incomparable assistance and clarifying presence, and for holding everything together.

To Maya Marshall and Maria Isabelle Carlos, the most generous, incisive, insightful, and wonderful editors, for trusting us from the beginning, for giving us space to explore, and for asking the questions that helped us shape this collection.

To Aricka Foreman, Jamie Kerry, Jim Plank, Jameka Williams and Haymarket Books for being a shining example of a press truly committed to changing the world.

To Rob Sato, for graciously sharing with us the artwork ("A New Sound") that is illuminating the cover of this anthology, and for the world he is creating with his beautiful, spellbinding art.

To Lawson Fusao Inada, whose books and poems we read at the very beginning of our apprenticeship to poetry, for his correspondence, stories, humor and grace.

To Hedi Mouchard, for collaborating with us and making us feel like family.

To Mitsuye Yamada, for offering us the most extraordinary example of how to be a poet in relation to history, to social justice, and to each other, and for ushering all of us into the experience of this work.

To Claire Kageyama-Ramakrishnan and Amy Uyematsu, luminous figures in the life of poetry, both of whom have passed into the spirit world; their work, which emanates in these pages, continues to shape and inspire us.

To all of the brilliant poets, writers, and artists who appear in the anthology, for entrusting us with truly astonishing and affirming work, and for helping us see and feel the extent of the beauty of the afterlife.

And to our ancestors—our parents and grandparents and great-grandparents, our aunts and uncles and great-aunts and great-uncles—

Love and thanks,

Brynn Saito and Brandon Shimoda, editors

Acknowledgments

Kiik Araki-Kawaguchi: "an ocean," "doorway of blossoms" and "evening song" published in *The Book of Kane and Margaret* by Kiik Araki-Kawaguchi © 2020 Kiik Araki-Kawaguchi. Published by FC2, an imprint of The University of Alabama Press. Used by permission from The University of Alabama Press.

Aaron Caycedo-Kimura: "Dad Called It *Camp*" published in *Shenandoah*, Volume 73, Number 2, Spring 2024.

Brian Komei Dempster: "Crossing," "Topaz," and "A Conversation with My Mother, Renko, About the Journey to and from Topaz Prison Camp in a Dream" from *Topaz*. Copyright © 2013 by Brian Komei Dempster. "Seized" from *Seize*. Copyright © 2020 by Brian Komei Dempster. All reprinted with the permission of The Permissions Company, LLC on behalf of Four Way Books.

Miya Folick: "Song for Kanjitsu" originally written for/performed at Densho Anniversary Gala, 2021.

Sesshu Foster: "Visitation" published in *Angry Days* (West End Press, 1987).

Steve Fujimura: "Fred Korematsu Day, Jan. 30" and "From Sam" from *Sad Asian Music*. Copyright © 2022 by Steve Fujimura. Reprinted with the permission of The Permissions Company, LLC on behalf of Finishing Line Press.

Richard Hamasaki: "Behind Barbed Wire—for Grandpa Senri Nao and Grandma Yoshino Nao" *From the Spider Bone Diaries: Poems and Songs* (University of Hawai'i Press, 2001).

Sharon Hashimoto: "Because You Showed Me a Piece of Barbed Wire," and "Reparations: My Mother and Heart Mountain" published in *The Crane Wife* (Story Line Press / Red Hen Press, 2021). "Smithsonian" published in *More American* (Grid Books, 2021).

Garrett Hongo: "Pilgrimage to the Shrine" from *Yellow Light* © 1982 by Garrett Hongo. Published by Wesleyan University Press, Middletown, CT. Used by permission. "Kubota to Miguel Hernandez in Heaven, Leupp, Arizona, 1942," and "Kubota to Nâzim Hikmet in Peredelkino, Moscow, from Leupp, Arizona" from *Coral Road: Poems* by Garrett Hongo, copyright © 2011 by Garrett Hongo. Used by permission of Alfred A. Knopf, an imprint of the Knopf Doubleday Publishing Group, a division of Penguin Random House LLC. All rights reserved.

Jodi Hottel: "A Few Seeds" published in *Heart Mountain* (Blue Light Press, 2012).

Kevin Irie: "Tashme" published in *Dinner at Madonna's* (Frontenac House, 2003). "The Camps: Burning the Dead" published in *Burning the Dead* (Wolsak and Wynn, 1992).

Erica H. Isomura: "A JC Cento, or why does silence become a shard?" published in *carte blanche* (issue 41, 2021). This cento is crafted with lines from the following: "Tegami" by Carolyn Nakagawa; "A Hundred and Fifty Pounds" by Michael Prior, *Burning Province* (McClelland & Stewart, 2020); "For Shizu" by Mona Oikawa, *All Names Spoken* (Sister Vision Press, 1992); "Echoes" by Laura Fukumoto (Feminist Space Camp, 2019); "Wheels" by Roy K. Kiyooka (Coach House Press, 1982); "alley/bird/ally" by Hiromi Goto (CBC Books, 2020); "powell street" by Rita Wong, *Forage* (Nightwood Editions, 2007); "Offerings" by Joy Kogawa (1985); "there was nothing festive about The Fair At The PNE in 1942" by Erica Hiroko Isomura (SFU Publications, 2018); "in flight" by Roy Miki, *Saving Face* (Turnstone Press, 1991); "untitled" by Angela Marian May; "untitled" by shō yamagusiku.

Kurt Yokoyama Ikeda: "Only what you can carry" published in "Nikkei Uncovered: a poetry column" in *Discover Nikkei: Japanese Migrants and Their Descendants.*

Lauren Emiko Ito: "Arrival As We" published in Quiet Lightning Literary Magazine.

Miya Iwataki: "GAMBARE!" published in *NCRR: The Grassroots Struggle for Japanese American Redress and Reparations* (UCLA Asian American Studies Center Press, 2018).

Claire Kageyama-Ramakrishnan. "Shadow Mountain" from *Shadow Mountain: Poems.* Copyright © 2008 by Claire Kageyama-Ramakrishnan. Reprinted with the permission of The Permissions Company, LLC on behalf of Four Way Books.

W. Todd Kaneko: "American Sentences," "ghost story," and "Legacies of Camp" published in *This is How the Bone Sings* (Black Lawrence Press, 2020).

traci kato-kiriyama: "fire, near fire" and "No Redress" published in *Navigating With(out) Instruments* (Writ Large Press, 2021).

Christine Kitano: "Gaman" and "1942: In Response to Executive Order 9066" published in *Sky Country* (BOA Editions, 2017). "1945: My Father Leaves Topaz Internment Camp, Utah" published in *Birds of Paradise* (Lynx House Press, 2011).

Garrett Kurai: "The Return" published in "Nikkei Uncovered: a poetry column" in *Discover Nikkei: Japanese Migrants and Their Descendants.*

Keiko Lane: "Grandfather Explains" published in *Knocking at the Door* (Birch Bench Press, 2011).

Alison Lubar: "For the No-Nos" published in *Hiroshima Day Anthology* (Moonstone Arts Center).

Mia Ayumi Malhotra: "To My Many Mothers, Issei and Nisei," "A History of Isako," and "Portrait of Isako in Wartime" from *Isako, Isako.* Copyright © 2018 by Mia Ayumi Malhotra. Reprinted with the permission of The Permissions Company LLC on behalf of Alice James Books, alicejamesbooks.org.

Ali Meyers-Ohki: "Spell Cast by Imagined Queer Ancestor at Amache" published in *Queer Rain Magazine* (Volume 2, 2022).

Emily Mitamura: "Self-Portrait as Contained Swarm" published in The Margins (Asian American Writers Workshop, July 2021).

Hikari Leilani Miya: "Five of Cups" was published as "Elegy" in *Forum Literary Magazine* (City College of San Francisco, Fall 2020).

James Fujinami Moore: "notes on the phrase shikata ga nai, written after a Colorado state representative says in 2017 that the internment camps were justified because 'in the heat of battle there isn't time to distinguish who is a citizen and who is not,' or: it cannot be helped." from *indecent hours*. Copyright © 2022 by James Fujinami Moore. Reprinted with the permission of The Permissions Company, LLC on behalf of Four Way Books.

Paulette "Tkl' Un Yeik" Moreno: "Earth's Aging" published in "Nikkei Uncovered: a poetry column" in *Discover Nikkei: Japanese Migrants and Their Descendants*.

David Mura: "An Argument: On 1942" and "Letters from Post Relocation Camp (1942-45)" published in After We Lost Our Way (EP Dutton, NY, 1989). "Internment Camp Psychology" published in *Angels for the Burning* (BOA Editions Limited, Rochester, NY, 2004).

Heather Nagami: "The Gift" published in *Hostile* (Chax Press, 2005).

Noriko Nakada: "Nakada Issei / Translated Into English / Means Lost in the Fields" published as "Family Haiku" in The *Tiger Moth Review* (Issue 4, 2020).

Greer Nakadegawa-Lee: "Plaything" published in "Nikkei Uncovered: a poetry column" in *Discover Nikkei: Japanese Migrants and Their Descendants*.

Carolyn Nakagawa: "Evacuation" was published in chapbook form in 2018 in collaboration with Kayla Isomura. "Tegami" was set to music by Nikkei composer Kara Gibbs and the resulting art song has been performed on three different occasions to date: in 2019, 2020, and 2023.

Tamiko Nimura: "Instructions to All Persons of Japanese Ancestry (an erasure)" published in "Found In the Public Domain" series (Heron Tree, December, 2016).

Mona Oikawa: "For Shizu" published in *All Names Spoken: Poetry and Prose* by Tamai Kobayashi and Mona Oikawa (Toronto: Sister Vision Press, 1992).

Michael Prior: "A Hundred and Fifty Pounds," and "Tashme" from *Burning Province: Poems* by Michael Prior, copyright © 2020 Michael Prior. Reprinted by permission of McClelland & Stewart, a division of Penguin Random House Canada Limited. All rights reserved. "Lines Written While Visiting the Valley Where the Camp Was" published in *Beloit Poetry Journal,* Vol 71, No 2. (2021). "The Border" published in *The Sewanee Review* (Spring 2022).

Brynn Saito: "Thirteen Ways of Looking at a Teacher Resource" and "Theses on the Philosophy of History" published in *Under a Future Sky* (Red Hen Press, 2023).

Brandon Shimoda: "Gila River" published in *The Desert* (The Song Cave, 2018).

Leanne Toshiko Simpson: "Tankas for a Buried Town" published in *The Ex-Puritan,* issue 49 (spring 2020).

Micah Tasaka: "Tree (why my father didn't teach me Japanese)" published in "Nikkei Uncovered: A poetry column" in *Discover Nikkei: Japanese Migrants and Their Descendants.*

George Uba: "Old Photo, 1942" published in *Breaking Silence, An Anthology of Contemporary Asian American Poets,* edited by Joseph Bruchac (The Greenfield Review Press, 1983). "Dawn in the Internment Camp at Heart Mountain" published in *Ploughshares,* Vol. 18, No. 1: Spring 1992.

Amy Uyematsu: "36 Views of Manzanar" published in *That Blue Trickster Time* (What Books Press, 2022).

Terry Watada: "Summer Stars" published in *The Mask* (Mawenzi Publishing House, Toronto ON 2023). "Moon Above the Ruins" published in *Ten Thousand Views of Rain* (Thistledown Press, Saskatoon SK 2001).

shō yamagushiku: "a vastness" from *shima: poems* by shō yamagushiku, Copyright © 2024 shō yamagushiku. Reprinted by permission of McClelland & Stewart, a division of Penguin Random House Canada Limited. All rights reserved.

Doug Yamamoto: "At Manzanar the Mountains" published in *Ayumi: A Japanese American Anthology* (1980).

Traise Yamamoto: "At Heart Mountain, 1942" published in *Premonitions: The Kaya Anthology of New Asian North American Poetry* (1995).

About the Contributors

Kiik Araki-Kawaguchi is the author of *The Book of Kane and Margaret* (FC2 / UAP), inspired by his maternal grandparents. These grandparents met at Tulare Assembly Center, married at Gila River camp, and were together for 70 years.

Brittany Arita is an art director and lettering artist. Her grandpa was incarcerated at Manzanar & Minidoka. Her grandma was incarcerated at Rohwer.

Aaron Caycedo-Kimura is the author of *Common Grace* (Beacon Press, 2022) and *Ubasute* (Slapering Hol Press, 2021). His honors include a MacDowell Fellowship, a Robert Pinsky Global Fellowship, and a St. Botolph Club Foundation Emerging Artist Award. His father, Tetsumi Joe Kimura, was incarcerated at the Santa Anita Racetrack, Jerome, and Tule Lake.

Brian Komei Dempster is a Sansei whose mother's family was incarcerated at Topaz concentration camp in Utah and whose grandfather was interned at the Department of Justice camp in Crystal City, Texas. His poetry collections are *Topaz* (Four Way Books, 2013) and *Seize* (Four Way Books, 2020).

Miya Folick is a musician and songwriter. Her records include *Roach* (2023), *Premonitions* (2018), and *Give It To Me* (2017), among many other collaborations and songs. She lives in Los Angeles. She had family members incarcerated in Minidoka.

Sesshu Foster's grandparents, Otokichi Agawa and Umeko Yamane Agawa, were farm workers in San Luis Obispo county. Three of their nine children died before 1941, and in 1942, the family was sent to the Tulare detention center, and from there to Gila River. Foster is writing a book about the family.

Sharon Fujimoto-Johnson is a fourth-generation Japanese American author-illustrator whose grandfather was incarcerated at Sand Island and Honouliuli in Hawai'i . Her children's books include *The Mochi Makers* and *Shell Song,* which was inspired by the shells her grandfather collected at Sand Island.

Steve Fujimura is a poet and the author of *Sad Asian Music.* His work engages with memory, history, loss, and family. His parents were born in camp at Poston, AZ. From San José, Steve currently lives in Berkeley, CA.

Laura K. Fukumoto is a poet living on unceded Musqueam, Squamish, and Tseil-Watuth lands. Vancouver was the birthplace of her grandfather, before the family's permanent displacement to Toronto. Laura's grandparents were incarcerated, and married, in Slocan, British Columbia. Born in 1921, Grandma Kay Fukumoto is celebrating her first published work.

Cathlin Goulding is an educator and curriculum designer. A former public school teacher, she codirects YURI Education Project, an education consultancy that helps PK-12 educators teach and tell Asian American histories. Her grandparents and mother were incarcerated at the Jerome and Gila River camps. She lives in Queens, New York.

Rebecca A. Green is a writer who lives and works in the San Francisco East Bay area. Her mother Mitsue Matsumune was incarcerated in Poston along with other family members. The experiences of biraciality and otherness have formed Rebecca's life and work.

Sansei poet and independent filmmaker and producer **Richard Hamasaki**'s San Francisco born and raised mother, Setsuko Nao [Hamasaki], was incarcerated with parents and siblings in a horse stall at the now defunct Tanforan Racetrack in San Bruno, CA. They were transported by train to a concentration camp in Topaz, Utah.

Sharon Hashimoto writes poems and short stories. Her mother's family (grandparents, aunts and uncles) was incarcerated at Heart Mountain. Her poetry books are *The Crane Wife* (Red Hen Press) and *More American* (Grid

Books), winner of the 2022 Washington State Book Award. *Stealing Home*, a story collection, was published by Grid Books, 2025.

Casey Hidekawa Lane/Levinski (Amache/Topaz descendant) is a Nikkei Jewish poet and ritual artist from Huichin (so-called Piedmont, CA). Their special interests include the past, the future and all that is sacred. Free Ainu Mosir! Free Ryūkyū! Free Palestine!

Garrett Hongo was born in Volcano, Hawaiʻi and grew up on Oʻahu and in Los Angeles. Forthcoming from Knopf is *Ocean of Clouds: Poems*. He is Distinguished Professor of Creative Writing at the University of Oregon. When he was young, his grandfather told him stories about being incarcerated in Leupp, Arizona.

Jodi Hottel is sansei, third generation Japanese American. During WWII, her mother's family was incarcerated at Heart Mountain, Wyoming. Her chapbook of poems about the incarceration, *Heart Mountain*, won the 2012 Blue Light Press Poetry Prize. Jodi has published four chapbooks and been published in numerous journals and anthologies.

Kurt Yokoyama Ikeda (he/him) is a park ranger by profession and spoken word poet by passion. As a Shin-Nisei and a descendant of Tuna Canyon, Santa Anita, Poston, Lordsburg, and Crystal City, he preserves the legacy of Minidoka. He lives in Idaho with his beloved wife, April, and baby May (Gosei).

Kevin Irie is a third generation Japanese-Canadian from Toronto. Both his parents and grandparents were originally from Vancouver. They were sent to the internment camp of Popoff-Slocan, in the British Columbia interior, then relocated east to Toronto following the end of the war.

Michael Ishii is a healer, artist, and community organizer. His mother and her family were incarcerated at Minidoka concentration camp and his upstate NY relatives were massacred during WWII. Much of his life has been devoted to the work of nonviolence and healing multigenerational trauma related to Japanese American WWII incarceration.

Erica H. Isomura is a writer, poet, and interdisciplinary artist. She was raised by a Cantonese Canadian mother and a sansei Japanese Canadian father on Qayqayt territories/New Westminster, BC. Her grandparents were incarcerated in Tashme and Greenwood, BC. Erica currently lives in Toronto/Tkaronto.

Lauren Emiko Ito is an American Gosei poet, researcher, and organizer whose art explores American concentration camps, ancestral healing, and the genealogy of home. Her grandparents, aunts, uncles, cousins and extended family members were forcibly incarcerated at Sand Island Internment Camp (HI), Minidoka (CA), Angel Island (CA), Ortiz Park in Santa Fe (NM), among others. As a San Francisco Arts Commission Artist Grantee, Lauren's latest project convenes Japanese American poets and visual artists to co-create a "love letter to our ancestors: past, present and future."

Susan Kiyo Ito's memoir, *I Would Meet You Anywhere,* was published by the Ohio State University Press in 2023. She is the sansei descendant of incarcerees in Amache and the daughter of a 442nd veteran. She currently lives in California.

Miya Iwataki's mother, Sadae Nomura Iwataki was incarcerated in Manzanar; her Dad Kuwashi was S/Sgt in the 100th/442nd. Miya was profoundly impacted by testimonies of Issei and Nisei at the CWRIC Hearings. Today with NP/NCRR, she's actively supporting Black Reparations. Her lifelong cultural and political activism are reflected in her poetry, writings and columns.

Claire Kageyama-Ramakrishnan is a poet. She passed away in 2016. She published three books of poetry: *Shadow Mountain* 影山 (Four Way Books, 2008), *Bears, Diamond and Crane* (Four Way Books, 2011), and *Vidya's Tree* (Bull City Press, 2019). Her father and his two brothers were incarcerated at Manzanar Internment Camp, California.

W. Todd Kaneko is the author of *This Is How the Bone Sings* (Black Lawrence 2020) and *The Dead Wrestler Elegies* (New Michigan Press 2023), and co-author of *Slash/Slash* (Diode 2021) and *Poetry: A Writer's Guide and Anthology* (Bloomsbury Academic 2024). His father and grandparents were incarcerated at Minidoka.

traci kato-kiriyama is a Sansei/Yonsei multidisciplinary artist, author, educator and community organizer based in the South Bay of Los Angeles on unceded Tongva land. Their parents and grandparents were incarcerated at Manzanar and Tule Lake. tkk is the author of *Signaling* (2010) and *Navigating With(out) Instruments* (2021).

Amanda Mei Kim is a Yonsei and Korean American writer and founder of KanshaHistory.org. Her Bachan, No-No Boy Jichan, mother, and two uncles were incarcerated at Poston and Tule Lake where their sister was born in 1946. Her writing has appeared in *Brick, LitHub, NYTimes, PANK, DiscoverNikkei, Common* and *Tayo*.

Christine Kitano is the author of the poetry collections *Birds of Paradise* and *Sky Country*. Her chapbook, *Dumb Luck & other poems*, won the Robert Phillips Poetry Chapbook Prize. She is the daughter of Harry Kitano, who was incarcerated at Topaz.

Aisuke Kondo, born and raised in Japan and currently based in Berlin, Germany, is an interdisciplinary artist. His work focuses on the history of discrimination against Asians in Western societies and his great-grandfather, who lived in the United States. His great-grandfather was incarcerated at Santa Anita and Topaz.

Garrett Kurai, is a Los Angeles native and NYU MFA graduate who has poems in JANM's "Nikkei Uncovered," Lotus Magazine, PennSound, and Skylight Books Podcast. "The Return" was written after a Phil Levine prompt. Garrett's aunts, Joanne and Alice, and his Uncle Thomas, were incarcerated at Poston's camp. His father, Shuichi, played taiko at 1975's Manzanar Pilgrimage.

Keiko Lane is an Okinawan American poet, memoirist, and psychotherapist. Her current projects explore the relationships between stories told and untold, silence, embodiment, and the transmission of memory. Her family was incarcerated at Manzanar, where her mother was born.

Katherine Terumi Laubscher is a mixed gosei writer and founder of the Japanese American cultural journal *Kioku*. Her great-aunt Dorothy Nagai was incarcerated at Heart Mountain; Katherine's poetry is dedicated to her memory.

Alison Lubar is a poet and educator; their grandfather, along with their Auntie and great-grandmother, were incarcerated at Tule Lake. Alison writes about being queer, nonbinary, and mixed-race, with a focus on intergenerational healing. Find out more about their work at alisonlubar.com.

Mia Ayumi Malhotra is the author of *Mothersalt* (Alice James Books, 2025); the chapbook *Notes from the Birth Year*; and *Isako Isako*, winner of the Alice James Award, Nautilus Gold Award, National Indie Excellence Award, and Maine Literary Award. Her grandparents and great-grandparents were incarcerated at Rohwer and Lordsburg.

Angela Marian May is a gosei writer, artist, and PhD Candidate (English and Cultural Studies, McMaster University). Her grandmother was interned in Greenwood, British Columbia. Her grandfather grew up in Vancouver throughout the 1940s, living just outside Powell Street, in the Downtown Eastside—because his mother, Angela's great grandmother, resisted the RCMP.

Ali Meyers-Ohki (she/her) is a writer of fiction, poetry, and screenplays based in Sacramento, California. Her work has been published by *Queer Rain Magazine*, *Voyage YA Magazine*, and *ANMLY*. She is the recipient of a 2022 Hedgebrook residency and a 2023 Walter Dean Meyers grant. Her grandparents met while incarcerated at Amache.

Emily Mitamura is a poet and scholar of race, gender, empire, and film. With commitments to women of color and Third World feminisms, their work takes up archival, relational, and bodily hauntings. Her family was incarcerated at Poston and Heart Mountain.

Hikari Leilani Miya is a poet from the Central Valley of California. Grandparents and relatives were incarcerated at Jerome, Arkansas.

Starr Sumie Miyata is a yonsei (fourth generation) multiracial Japanese American, living, writing and working in Tokyo. She is often in Hiroshima, her great-grandfather Kyoichi's birthplace. Kyoichi, a first generation Japanese settler in Hawai'i, was incarcerated at Sand Island, Angel Island, Fort Sill, Camp Livingston, Fort Missoula, and Jerome.

James Fujinami Moore is a poet born and raised in Los Angeles. His great-uncles were incarcerated at Jerome prior to serving in the 442nd.

Paulette "Tkl' Un Yeik" Moreno is a civil rights leader, poet, and speaker. Her grandfather, George Kamachi Miyasato Sr, and her Uncle George Miyasato Jr, were incarcerated during World War II in Lordsburg, NM and Minidoka. Paulette and Harriet Miyasato Beleal, her mother, are journeying to share their vision of truth that reflects Worth.

David Mura is the author of the memoirs *Turning Japanese* and *Where the Body Meets Memory*; the poetry collections *After We Lost Our Way, The Colors of Desire, Angels for the Burning,* and *The Last Incantations*; the novel *Famous Suicides of the Japanese Empire*; the essay collection, *The Stories Whiteness Tells Itself*; and the documentary *MIS Nisei Armed With Language*. His mother was incarcerated in Minidoka and his father was incarcerated in Jerome.

Yukiko Nagakura (she/her) is an interdisciplinary artist who lives and works in Berlin. In 2017 and 2019, she visited several of the incarceration camps with her spouse, Aisuke Kondo. This experience sparked her interest in learning about the history of Japanese immigration to the United States, with a specific focus on women.

Heather Nagami is a yonsei (fourth generation) Japanese American poet from Southern California. She is the author of *Hostile* (Chax Press). Her father's side of the family was incarcerated at Jerome and Rohwer. Her mother's side, the Togawa family, was incarcerated at Poston.

Noriko Nakada is a multi-racial Asian American who creates fiction, nonfiction, and poetry to capture the hidden stories she has been told not to talk about. Her father was incarcerated during World War II at both Heart

Mountain and Gila Rivers. Noriko is represented by Emily Keyes of Keyes Agency.

Greer Nakadegawa-Lee is an illustrator and poet from Oakland, California. You can find more of her work at greernl.weebly.com. Members of her family were incarcerated in Poston and Manzanar. Her uncle, Art Nomura, wrote the novel *Mizuko: True Spirit,* detailing his grandmother's time in Manzanar, where he was born.

Carolyn Nakagawa is a fourth-generation Anglo-Japanese Canadian poet and playwright who makes her home in the territory colonized as Vancouver, British Columbia. Her paternal grandparents were forcibly uprooted from Steveston and lived in Magna Bay and Westbank before returning to Vancouver in 1950.

Ryan Hitoshi Nakano is an Okinawan/Japanese American poet, journalist and aspiring birder currently living in Huchiun (aka Oakland, CA) on the unceded lands of the Lisjan Ohlone with his wonderful partner and cat. His paternal grandfather was incarcerated at Amache (Granada) and paternal grandmother at Topaz.

Tamiko Nimura is an Asian American (Sansei/Pinay) creative nonfiction writer and public historian, originally from California and now living in Washington State. Her father and eight of her family members were incarcerated at Tule Lake. She is a board member of the Tule Lake Committee. Her forthcoming memoir is *A Place For What We Lose: A Daughter's Return to Tule Lake.*

Mona Oikawa is a faculty member at York University and lives on the territory care taken by the Anishinabek Nation, the Haudenosaunee Confederacy, and the Wendat, and the current treaty holders, the Mississaugas of the Credit First Nation. She is the author of *Cartographies of Violence: Japanese Canadian Women, Memory, and the Subjects of the Internment.* Her mother and maternal grandmother Shizu were incarcerated in the Slocan, BC camp. Her father was incarcerated in the Schreiber, ON Camp and her paternal grandmother was incarcerated in the Tashme, BC camp.

Troy Osaki, the descendant of Filipino and Japanese immigrants, is a poet, organizer, and attorney. His grandmother was incarcerated at the Puyallup Assembly Center and the Minidoka War Relocation Center. After two years of separation, his grandmother reunited with her father at the Crystal City Alien Enemy Detention Facility.

Michael Prior is a poet and teacher. His grandparents and their families were incarcerated in Tashme, a camp located on the unceded land of the Coast Salish peoples. Prior's most recent book of poems, *Burning Province*, won the 2021 BC & Yukon Book Prize for poetry and the 2020 Canada-Japan Literary Award.

Brynn Saito's third collection of poetry, *Under a Future Sky* (Red Hen Press, 2023), was inspired by her visit with her father to Gila River, the place where her aunt, grandparents, and other family members were incarcerated. Brynn teaches at California State University, Fresno.

Rob Sato is an artist based in Los Angeles. His grandfather was incarcerated in the Jerome and Rohwer, Arkansas camps.

Brandon Shimoda is the author of several books of poetry and prose, including *The Grave on the Wall* and *The Afterlife Is Letting Go*, both from City Lights. He had family in Heart Mountain, Poston, and Fort Missoula, where his grandfather was incarcerated under suspicion of being a spy for Japan.

Patrick Shiroishi is a multi-instrumentalist and composer living in Los Angeles. His grandparents, Hidemi Pat & Sayoko Dorothy Shiroishi, were incarcerated at Tule Lake. Their story is special as they met and married each other in the camps. It is a reminder that even in the darkest of moments, light and hope can still shine through.

Leanne Toshiko Simpson is a mixed-race Yonsei writer and psychiatric survivor. Her maternal grandparents were interned in Slocan Valley. Leanne teaches creative writing at the University of Toronto and cofounded Mata Ashita, an intergenerational writing workshop for Japanese Canadians. Her debut novel *Never Been Better* explores mental health from cross-cultural perspectives.

Dana Swensen is a poet and writer who lives in California. Her great grandfather, an Issei man who chose to leave his family behind in Hawai'i, was incarcerated from January of 1942, first on the island Lanai, then a POW camp in Texas, and then the Santa Fe Internment Camp for the duration of the war.

Kenneth Tanemura teaches writing at the University of Central Florida. His poems have appeared in *The Iowa Review, The Cincinnati Review, New Ohio Review, South Florida Poetry Journal*, and elsewhere. Kenneth's father is a Sansei Kibei who was interned at Gila River and Tule Lake.

Micah Tasaka (田坂舞花) is a queer, nonbinary poet, multidisciplinary artist, and reiki master from Colton, California. Their grandmother was incarcerated at Poston, AZ, and their grandfather fought in the 442nd Infantry Regiment in WWII. They are the author of *Expansions* (Jamii Publishing, 2017). Currently, Micah is earning their MFA in poetry from the University of New Orleans and working for the Rainbow Pride Youth Alliance as the Director of the Inland Empire's first LGBTQ+ Youth Drop in Center. Visit www.micahtasaka.com

George Uba is Professor Emeritus of English, CSU Northridge. Literary & cultural critic, poet, and memoirist. Author of the books *Disorient Ballroom* and *Water Thicker Than Blood*, which traced the generational impacts of his parents' wartime incarceration at Heart Mountain. Finalist for the 2024 Pablo Neruda Prize for Poetry. Recent poems in *New England Review, Michigan Quarterly Review, Nimrod*, and *Atlanta Review.*

Amy Uyematsu was a renowned sansei poet whose family was incarcerated in Manzanar and Gila River. She is the author of *30 Miles From J-Town, Nights of Fire, Nights of Rain, Stone Bow Prayer, The Yellow Door, Basic Vocabulary* and *That Blue Trickster Time*. While at UCLA's Asian American Studies Center, she co-edited the first widely used Asian American Studies anthology, *Roots: An Asian American Reader* (1971). Amy penned the widely acclaimed essay, "The Emergence of Yellow Power" (Gidra, 1969), an assertion of Asian American identity. Her poems consider the intersection of politics, mathematics, spirituality and the natural world. Amy died of breast cancer in 2023.

Terry Watada is a well-published writer living in Canada. He has four novels, six poetry books, and a collection of short stories in print. *Hiroshima Bomb Money* is his latest novel. He is honoured that his two poems in this collection were selected for inclusion. In 1942, his father was forced to join a road gang before reuniting with his family in Minto BC, a self-sustaining internment camp.

Anne Yukie Watanabe (she/her) is a queer femme yonsei and shin-nisei nurse, organizer, peer counselor and writer living in Chicago. Her grandparents were incarcerated in Tashme and Lillooet in Canada. She is a founding member of Nikkei Uprising, a Nikkei group that organizes for collective liberation with an abolitionist and anti-imperialist lens.

Syd Westley is a poet and artist in Berkeley, CA. Their grandparents were incarcerated at Minidoka and Tule Lake.

shō yamagushiku writes against the imperial inheritances that breathe life into the word "nikkei." His first poetry collection entitled *shima* reflects ancestors, violence, and tradition. He is located on the homelands of the Lekwungen and W̱SÁNEĆ peoples (Victoria, BC).

Doug Yamamoto is a retired union construction worker enjoying the benefits of being a longtime union member of Glaziers Union #718. His mother was imprisoned at Poston, along with her relatives, and his father incarcerated at Amache, along with his parents and siblings.

Traise Yamamoto is Associate Professor of English at the University of California, Riverside. She is the author of *Masking Selves, Making Subjects: Japanese American Women, Identity, and the Body*. Her mother and family were incarcerated at Tule Lake; her grandfather was also separately imprisoned at Santa Fe. Her father and family were incarcerated at Heart Mountain; her uncle was found guilty of draft evasion and imprisoned on McNeil Island. Her father, David Hiroshi Yamamoto, testified during the Redress and Reparations hearings.

May these poems
serve to enhance
the history.

Lawson Fusao Inada

About Haymarket Books

Haymarket Books is a radical, independent, nonprofit book publisher based in Chicago. Our mission is to publish books that contribute to struggles for social and economic justice. We strive to make our books a vibrant and organic part of social movements and the education and development of a critical, engaged, and internationalist Left.

We take inspiration and courage from our namesakes, the Haymarket Martyrs, who gave their lives fighting for a better world. Their 1886 struggle for the eight-hour day—which gave us May Day, the international workers' holiday—reminds workers around the world that ordinary people can organize and struggle for their own liberation. These struggles—against oppression, exploitation, environmental devastation, and war—continue today across the globe.

Since our founding in 2001, Haymarket has published more than nine hundred titles. Radically independent, we seek to drive a wedge into the risk-averse world of corporate book publishing. Our authors include Angela Y. Davis, Arundhati Roy, Keeanga-Yamahtta Taylor, Eve Ewing, Aja Monet, Mariame Kaba, Naomi Klein, Rebecca Solnit, Olúfẹ́mi O. Táíwò, Mohammed El-Kurd, José Olivarez, Noam Chomsky, Winona LaDuke, Robyn Maynard, Leanne Betasamosake Simpson, Howard Zinn, Mike Davis, Marc Lamont Hill, Dave Zirin, Astra Taylor, and Amy Goodman, among many other leading writers of our time. We are also the trade publishers of the acclaimed Historical Materialism Book Series.

Haymarket also manages a vibrant community organizing and event space in Chicago, Haymarket House, the popular Haymarket Books Live event series and podcast, and the annual Socialism Conference.

Also by Haymarket Books

All the Blood Involved in Love, Maya Marshall

Ankle-Deep in Pacific Water, E. Hughes

Build Yourself a Boat, Camonghne Felix

Citizen Illegal, José Olivarez

I Remember Death by Its Proximity to What I Love, Mahogany L. Browne

Like a Hammer: Poets on Mass Incarceration, edited by Diana Marie Delgado

A Map of My Want, Faylita Hicks

Nazar Boy, Tarik Dobbs

O Body, Dan "Sully" Sullivan

Rifqa, Mohammed El-Kurd

Super Sad Black Girl, Diamond Sharp

There Are Trans People Here, H. Melt

Too Much Midnight, Krista Franklin

We the Gathered Heat: Asian American and Pacific Islander Poetry, Performance, and Spoken Word, edited by Franny Choi, Bao Phi, No'u Revilla, and Terisa Siagatonu,

www.ingramcontent.com/pod-product-compliance
Lightning Source LLC
LaVergne TN
LVHW091635100826
845152LV00002B/46

* 9 7 8 8 4 9 9 5 3 6 9 9 6 *